D1649581

THE CROSS
AND THE
SWITCH-
BLADE

YOUNG READER'S EDITION

THE CROSS
AND THE
SWITCH-
BLADE

DAVID WILKERSON
WITH JOHN AND ELIZABETH SHERRILL

ABRIDGED BY LONNIE HULL DUPONT
ILLUSTRATED BY TIM FOLEY

Chosen

a division of Baker Publishing Group
Minneapolis, Minnesota

© 1963, 2000, 2008 by David Wilkerson
© 2018 by Global Teen Challenge and World Challenge

Published by Chosen Books
11400 Hampshire Avenue South
Bloomington, Minnesota 55438
www.chosenbooks.com

Chosen Books is a division of
Baker Publishing Group, Grand Rapids, Michigan

Printed in the United States of America

All rights reserved. No part of this publication may be reproduced, stored in a retrieval system, or transmitted in any form or by any means—for example, electronic, photocopy, recording—without the prior written permission of the publisher. The only exception is brief quotations in printed reviews.

ISBN 978-0-8007-9879-6
Library of Congress Control Number: 2017963563

Text abridged by Lonnie Hull DuPont

Unless otherwise indicated, Scripture is taken from the King James Version of the Bible.

Scripture marked NEB is taken from *The New English Bible*. Copyright © 1961, 1970, 1989 by The Delegates of Oxford University Press and The Syndics of the Cambridge University Press. Reprinted by permission.

Cover design by Studio Gearbox
Interior illustrations by Tim Foley

20 21 22 23 24   7 6 5 4 3 2

In keeping with biblical principles of creation stewardship, Baker Publishing Group advocates the responsible use of our natural resources. As a member of the Green Press Initiative, our company uses recycled paper when possible. The text paper of this book is composed in part of post-consumer waste.

green press INITIATIVE

To my wife, Gwen

1

This whole strange adventure got its start late one night when I was reading *Life* magazine and turned a page.

At first glance, it seemed that there was nothing on the page to interest me. It carried a pen drawing of a trial taking place in New York City, 350 miles away. I'd never been to New York, and I never wanted to go, except to see the Statue of Liberty.

As I started to flip the page over, my attention was caught by the eyes of one of the figures in the drawing. A boy. One of seven teenage boys on trial for murder. The artist had caught such a look of bewilderment and hatred and despair in his features that I opened the magazine wider to get a closer look. As I did, I began to cry.

"What's the matter with me!" I said aloud. I looked at the picture more carefully. The boys were members of a gang called the Dragons. Beneath their picture was the story of how they had brutally attacked and killed a fifteen-year-old polio victim named Michael Farmer. The seven boys

stabbed Michael in the back seven times with their knives, then beat him over the head with belts. They went away wiping blood through their hair.

The story turned my stomach. In our little mountain town such things seemed unbelievable.

That's why I was dumbfounded by a thought that sprang suddenly into my head—full-blown, as though it had come into me from somewhere else.

Go to New York City and help those boys.

I laughed out loud. "Me?"

Go to New York City and help those boys. The thought was still there, vivid as ever.

"I'd be a fool. I know nothing about kids like that."

But the idea would not go away: I was to go to New York, and I was to go now, while the trial was in progress.

Until I turned that page, mine had been a predictable but satisfying life. The little mountain church that I served in Philipsburg, Pennsylvania, had grown slowly but steadily. We had a new church building, a new parsonage, a swelling missionary budget.

My wife, Gwen, and I were happy in Philipsburg. The life of a country preacher suited me. Most of our parishioners were either farmers or coal workers, honest, God-fearing and generous. They brought in tithes of canned goods, butter, eggs, milk, and meat. They were people you could admire and learn from.

Gwen and I worked hard in Philipsburg. By New Year's Day, 1958, there were 250 people in the parish—including Bonnie, our new little daughter.

But I was restless. I was feeling a kind of spiritual discontent that wasn't satisfied by looking at the new church

building or the swelling missionary budget or the crowd-
ing in the pews. I remember the night I recognized it. It
was February 9, 1958. On that night I decided to sell my
television set.

Gwen and the children were asleep when the idea came
to me, and I was sitting in front of the set watching the
Late Show.

*What would happen if I sold that TV set and spent that
time—two hours a night—praying?*

Right away I thought of objections to the idea. I was tired
at night. I needed the relaxation. Television was part of
our culture; it wasn't good for a minister to be out of touch
with what people were seeing and talking about.

I got up from my chair and stood at my window looking
out over the moonlit hills. Then I bowed my head. I made
an experiment in a special kind of prayer that seeks to find
God's will through a sign. "Putting a fleece before the Lord,"
it is called, because Gideon, when he was trying to find God's
will for his life, asked for a sign. He placed a lamb's fleece on
the ground and asked Him to send down dew everywhere
but there. In the morning, the ground was soaked with dew,
but Gideon's fleece was dry: God had granted him a sign.

"Jesus," I said, "I'm going to put an ad for that TV set
in the paper. If You're behind this idea, let a buyer appear
right away—within an hour . . . within half an hour . . .
after the paper gets on the streets."

I made it pretty hard on God, because I really didn't
want to give up television.

When I told Gwen about my decision next morning, she
was unimpressed. "Half an hour!" she said. "Sounds to me
like you don't want to do all that praying."

Gwen had a point, but I put the ad in the paper anyhow. It was a comical scene in our living room after the paper appeared. I sat on the sofa with the television set looking at me from one side, the children and Gwen looking at me from another, and my eyes on a great big alarm clock beside the telephone.

Twenty-nine minutes passed.

"Well, Gwen," I said, "it looks like you're right. I guess I won't have to—"

The telephone rang.

I picked it up slowly.

"You have a TV set for sale?" a man's voice asked.

"That's right. An RCA in good condition. Nineteen-inch screen, two years old."

"How much do you want for it?"

"One hundred dollars," I said.

"I'll take it," the man said.

"You don't even want to look at it?"

"No. Have it ready in fifteen minutes. I'll bring the money."

My life changed. Every night at midnight, instead of flipping channels, I stepped into my office, closed the door, and began to pray. At first the time seemed to drag and I grew restless.

Then I learned how to make Bible reading a part of my prayer life. I'd never read the Bible through, including all the begats. I learned how important it is to strike a balance between prayers of petition and prayers of praise. What a wonderful thing it is to spend a solid hour just being thankful. It throws all of life into a new perspective.

It was during one of these late evenings of prayer that I picked up *Life* magazine.

I'd been fidgety all night. Gwen and the children were in Pittsburgh visiting grandparents. I had been at prayer for a long time. I felt particularly close to God, and yet for reasons I could not understand I also felt a heavy sadness. I wondered what it could possibly mean. I felt uneasy, as though I had received orders but could not make out what they were.

I got up and walked around the study. On my desk lay a copy of *Life*. I reached over to pick it up, then caught myself. No, I wasn't going to fall into that trap—reading a magazine when I was supposed to be praying.

I started prowling around the office, and each time I came to the desk my attention was drawn to that magazine.

"Lord, is there something in there You want me to see?" I said aloud.

I sat down in my desk chair and opened the magazine. A moment later I was looking at a pen drawing of seven boys, and tears were streaming down my face.

The next night was Wednesday prayer meeting at church. I decided to tell the congregation about my new twelve-to-two prayer experiment, and about the strange suggestion that had come out of it.

Wednesday night turned out to be a cold, snowy evening. Not many people showed up, and those who did get out straggled in late and sat in the back, which is always a bad sign to a preacher.

I didn't preach a sermon that night. Instead I asked everyone to come down close "because I have something I want to show you," I said. I opened *Life* and held it down for them to see.

"Take a good look at the faces of these boys," I said. Then

I told them how I had burst into tears and how I had gotten the clear instruction to go to New York, myself, and try to help those boys. My parishioners looked at me stonily.

Then an amazing thing happened. I told the congregation that I wanted to go to New York, but that I had no money. Although there were so few people present, my parishioners silently came forward that evening and one by one placed an offering on the Communion table. The offering amounted to 75 dollars, enough to get to New York City and back by car.

Early Thursday morning I climbed into my car with Miles Hoover, the youth director from church, and backed out of the driveway. I kept asking myself why in the world I was going to New York, carrying a page torn out of *Life*.

I kept asking myself why the faces of those boys made me choke up, even now, whenever I looked at them.

"I'm afraid, Miles," I confessed, as we sped along the Pennsylvania Turnpike.

"Afraid?"

"That I may be doing something foolhardy."

We drove in silence for a while.

"Miles?" I kept my eyes straight ahead, embarrassed to look at him. "Get your Bible and open it at random and read me the first passage you put your finger on."

Miles looked at me as if to accuse me of practicing some kind of superstitious rite, but he reached into the back seat and got his Bible. Out of the corner of my eye I watched him close his eyes, open the book, and plunge his finger onto a spot on the page.

He read to himself, then turned to look at me.

The passage was in the 126th Psalm, verses five and six. "'They that sow in tears,'" Miles read, "'shall reap in joy. He that goeth forth and weepeth, bearing precious seed, shall doubtless come again with rejoicing, bringing his sheaves with him.'"

We were greatly encouraged as we drove on toward New York. It was a good thing, because it was the last encouragement we were to receive for a long time.

2

We came into the outskirts of New York along Route 46, which connects the New Jersey Turnpike with the George Washington Bridge.

We needed gasoline, so we pulled into a station just short of the bridge. While Miles stayed with the car, I went into a phone booth and called the district attorney named in the *Life* article. When I reached the proper office, I tried to sound like a dignified pastor. The prosecutor's office was not impressed.

"The district attorney will not put up with any interference in this case. Good day to you, sir."

The line went dead.

I stepped out of the phone booth and tried to recapture my feeling of mission. It was getting dark.

"Hey, David," Miles called. "We're blocking the exit here."

We pulled out onto the highway. Instantly we were locked in a gigantic traffic flow; we couldn't have turned around if we'd wanted to. I had never seen so many cars, all in a hurry. They pulled around me and honked.

What a sight the bridge was! A river of red lights on the right—the taillights of the cars in front—and the white glare of oncoming traffic and the immense skyline looming ahead. I realized how countrified I really was.

"What do we do now?" I asked Miles at the end of the bridge. A dozen green signs pointed us to highways whose names meant nothing to us.

"When in doubt," said Miles, "follow the car ahead."

The car ahead, it turned out, was going to upper Manhattan. So did we.

"Look!" said Miles, after we had gone through two red lights and nearly run over a police officer who stood shaking his head after us. "There's a name I know! Broadway!"

A few blocks later, we came to Macy's, then Gimbels. My heart leaped at the sight of them. Here were names I knew. Gwen ordered things from these stores.

"Let's look for a hotel near here," I suggested.

Across the street was the Hotel Martinique; we decided on that. Now there was the problem of parking. There was a car lot across from the hotel, but when the man at the gate told us the price, I backed into the street again.

"It's because we're from out of town," I told Miles as I drove away with what I hoped was indignant speed. "They think they can get away with anything if you're a stranger."

Half an hour later we were back at the parking lot. "All right, you win," I said to the man, who didn't smile. A few minutes later, we were in our room on the twelfth floor of the Martinique. I stood at the window, looking down at the people and cars below. Every now and again a gust of wind blew clouds of trash and newspaper around the corner.

A group of teenagers were huddled around an open fire across the street. They were dancing in the cold, holding out their hands to the blaze.

"I'm going to try the district attorney's office again," I said to Miles. I knew I was making a nuisance of myself, but I could think of no other way to reach those boys. I called several times. At last I annoyed someone into giving me some information.

"Look," I was told, "the only person who can give you permission to see those boys is Judge Davidson himself."

"How do I get to see Judge Davidson?"

"He'll be at the trial tomorrow morning. One hundred Court Street. Now good-bye, Reverend. Please don't call here again."

I tried to call Judge Davidson. But the operator told me his line had been disconnected.

We went to bed, but I did not sleep. I divided the long hours between wondering what I was doing here and fervent prayers of thanks that, whatever it was, it couldn't keep me here long.

The next morning, shortly after seven o'clock, Miles and I checked out of the hotel. We decided to fast and skipped breakfast.

If we had known New York better, we would have taken the subway downtown to the courthouse. But we didn't know New York, so we got our car out of the lot and once again headed down Broadway.

One hundred Court Street was a mammoth building. It attracted hundreds every day who had business there, but it also drew curious, gawking spectators. One man in particular that day was sounding off outside the courtroom where the Michael Farmer trial was to reconvene later in the morning.

"Electric chair's too good for them," he said to the public. "Got to teach young punks a lesson. Make an example out of them."

By the time we arrived, there were forty people waiting in line to enter the courtroom. I discovered later that there were 42 seats available that day in the spectator section. If we'd stopped for breakfast, all that has happened to me since the morning of February 28, 1958, might have taken a different direction.

For ninety minutes we stood in line, not daring to leave. Once, when a court official passed down the line, I pointed to a door down the corridor.

"Is that Judge Davidson's chambers?" I asked.

He nodded.

"Could I see him, do you think?"

The man looked at me, laughed, and walked away.

At ten o'clock a guard opened the courtroom doors, and we filed into a vestibule where each one of us was inspected.

"They've threatened the judge," said the man in front of me. "The Dragon gang. Said they'd get him in court."

Miles and I took the last two seats. I found myself next to the man who thought that justice should be faster. He gave me a running commentary on court procedure. When a group of men strolled in from the back of the court, I was informed these were the court-appointed lawyers.

"Twenty-seven of them," my friend said. "Had to be supplied by the state. Nobody else would defend the scum. They had to plead 'not guilty.' State law for first-degree murder."

Then the boys themselves came in.

I don't know what I'd been expecting. Men, I suppose. After all this was a murder trial. But these were children. Seven scared children on trial for their lives for a merciless killing. The seven boys, each handcuffed to a guard, were escorted to the left of the room, then seated and the handcuffs taken off.

A girl took the stand.

"That's the gang's doll," said my neighbor.

She was shown a knife and asked if she recognized it. She admitted that it was the knife from which she had wiped blood on the night of the murder. It took all morning to achieve that statement.

Then suddenly, the proceedings were over. It took me by surprise—which may, in part, explain what happened next. I didn't have time to think over what I was going to do.

I saw Judge Davidson stand and announce that the court was adjourned. In my mind's eye I saw him leaving that room and disappearing forever.

"I'm going up there to talk to him," I whispered to Miles.

The judge was gathering his robes together, preparing to leave. I grasped my Bible in my right hand, hoping it would identify me as a minister, and ran to the front of the room.

"Your Honor!" I called.

Judge Davidson whirled around.

"Your Honor, please, would you respect me as a minister and let me have an audience with you?"

By now the guards had reached me. I suppose the fact that the judge's life had been threatened was responsible for some of the roughness that followed. Two of the guards picked me up by the elbows and hustled me up the aisle. There was a sudden scurrying and shouting in the press

section as photographers raced past each other trying to get pictures.

The guards turned me over to two policemen in the vestibule.

A policeman addressed me. "All right, mister. Where's the gun?"

I assured him that I didn't have a gun. Once again I was searched.

"Who were you with?"

"Miles Hoover, our youth director."

They brought Miles in. He was shaken, more with anger than with fear.

Some of the press managed to get into the room while the police questioned us. I showed the police my ordination papers so they'd know I was truly a clergyman. They were arguing among themselves about what charges to book me on. The sergeant said he'd find out Judge Davidson's wishes, and while he was gone the reporters pumped me with questions.

The sergeant came back saying that Judge Davidson didn't want to press charges. They would let me go this time if I agreed never to come back.

"Don't worry," said Miles. "He won't come back."

They escorted me brusquely out to the corridor. There a semicircle of newsmen were waiting with their cameras cocked. One man said, "Hey, Rev'ren. What's that book you got there?"

"My Bible."

"Hold it up where we can see it."

I was naïve enough to hold it up. Flashbulbs popped, and suddenly I knew how it would come out in the papers: A

Bible-waving country preacher, with his hair standing up on his head, interrupts a murder trial.

As soon as they let us go, we hurried to the parking lot, where our car had earned another charge. Miles didn't say a word. Once we got in the car and closed the door, I bowed my head and cried for twenty minutes.

Going back over the George Washington Bridge, I turned and looked once more at the New York skyline. I remembered the passage from Psalms that had given us so much encouragement: "They that sow in tears shall reap in joy."

What kind of guidance had that been? How would I face my wife, my parents, my church? I had stood before the congregation and told them that God had moved on my heart. Now I must tell them I had made a mistake and did not know the heart of God at all.

3

iles," I said, when the bridge was fifty miles behind us, "do you mind if we drive home by way of Scranton?" My parents lived there. I wanted, frankly, to cry on their shoulders a bit.

By the time we reached Scranton the next morning, the story and my photo were in the newspapers. The Michael Farmer trial was well covered by the press, but news items on it had begun to run scarce. The grisly aspects of the murder had been explored until the last ounce of horror had been wrung from them. Now a bizarre sidelight appeared, and the papers made the most of it.

I worried how my parents would be affected by this. I was eager to see them, but now I dreaded the moment of meeting. After all, the name I had exposed to ridicule was theirs also.

"Maybe," said Miles as we turned into their driveway, "they won't have seen it."

They had seen it. A newspaper was spread out on the kitchen table, turned to the account of the wild-eyed,

Bible-waving young preacher who had been thrown out of the Michael Farmer murder trial.

"David," Mother said, "what a . . . pleasant surprise."

"Hello, son," said Dad.

I sat down. Miles had tactfully gone for a walk.

I nodded my head toward the newspaper. "I'll say it for you. How are we ever going to live this down?"

"Well, son," my father said, "it's not so much us. You could lose your ordination."

Realizing his concern for me, I kept silent.

"What are you going to do when you get back to Philipsburg, David?" Mother asked.

"I haven't thought that far yet."

Mother went to the refrigerator and got out a bottle of milk.

"Do you mind if I give you a piece of advice?" she asked, pouring me a glass. Often, when Mother was ready to give me advice, she didn't stop to ask my permission. This time, though, she waited, milk bottle in hand, until I nodded my head.

"When you get back home, David, don't be too quick to say you were wrong. 'The Lord moves in mysterious ways His wonders to perform.' It's possible this is all part of a plan you can't see from where you're standing. I have always believed in your good judgment."

All the way back to Philipsburg I mulled over Mother's words.

I took Miles to his house and then drove to the parsonage. The telephone kept ringing for the next three days. One of the town officials called to bawl me out. Fellow ministers told me they thought it was cheap publicity. When I finally dared to walk downtown, heads turned to follow me all along the street. One man who was always trying to bring more business into town pumped my hand and slapped me on the back and said, "Say, Reverend, you really put Philipsburg on the map!"

Hardest of all was meeting my parishioners that Sunday. They were polite—and silent. From the pulpit that morning I looked at the problem as squarely as I could.

"I know all of you must have questions," I said. "You must be asking yourselves, 'What kind of egoist do we have for a preacher, a man who thinks that every whim he gets is a mandate from God?' This is a legitimate question. It would surely look as though I had confused my own will for God's.

"And yet, let's ask ourselves: If it is true that the job of us humans here on earth is to do the will of God, can we not expect that in some way He will make that will known to us?"

Stony faces, still.

But the congregation was remarkably kind. Most of the people said they thought I had acted foolishly, but that they knew my heart was in the right place. One good lady said, "We still want you even if nobody else does." After that memorable statement, she *did* spend a long time explaining that she hadn't meant it to sound like that.

Then a strange thing happened.

In my nightly prayer sessions, Romans 8:28 came into my mind again and again: "All things work together for good to them that love God, to them who are the called according to his purpose."

It came with great force and a sense of reassurance.

Along with it came an idea so preposterous that for several nights I dismissed it as soon as it appeared.

Go back to New York.

I tried ignoring it three nights in a row and found it as persistent as ever. So I set about to deal with it. This time I was prepared.

New York, in the first place, was clearly not my cup of tea. I did not like the place, and I was unsuited for life there. I revealed my ignorance at every turn, and the very name *New York* was for me now a symbol of embarrassment. I was not going to drive eight hours there and eight hours back for the privilege of making a fool of myself again.

As for going back to the congregation with a new request for money, it was out of the question. These farmers and mine workers were already giving more than they should. How would I explain it to them, when I myself did not understand this fresh order to return to the scene of my defeat? Wild horses couldn't drag me to my church with such a suggestion.

And yet, so persistent was this new idea that on Wednesday night, I asked my parishioners for more money to get me back to New York.

Their response was truly amazing. One by one, they again marched down the aisle and placed an offering on the Communion table. This time, there were more people in the church, perhaps 150. But the interesting thing is that the offering was the same. When the dimes and quarters and bills were counted, there was just enough—again. Seventy dollars had been collected.

The next morning Miles and I were on our way by six. We took the same route, stopped at the same gas station, took the bridge into New York. Crossing the bridge, I prayed,

Lord, I do not ask to be shown Your purpose, only that You direct my steps.

Once again we found Broadway and turned south along this only route we knew. We were driving slowly along when suddenly I had the strongest feeling that I should get out of the car.

"I'm going to find a place to park," I said to Miles. "I want to walk around for a while." We found an empty meter.

"I'll be back in a while, Miles. I don't even know what it is I'm looking for."

I left Miles in the car and started walking down the street. I hadn't gone half a block before I heard a voice: "Hey, Davie!"

I didn't turn around at first, thinking some boy was calling a friend.

"Hey, Davie. Preacher!"

This time I did turn around. A group of six teenage boys were leaning against the side of a building, smoking. A seventh boy separated himself from the group and walked after me. I liked his smile as he spoke.

"Aren't you the preacher they kicked out of the Michael Farmer trial?"

"Yes. How'd you know?"

"Your picture was all over the place. Your face is kind of easy to remember."

"You know my name, but I don't know yours."

"I'm Tommy. I'm the president of the Rebels."

I asked Tommy if those were his friends, and he offered to introduce me.

"Hey, fellows," he said, "here's the preacher who was kicked out of the Farmer trial."

One by one, the boys came up to inspect me. Only one boy did not budge. He flicked open a knife and began to carve an unprintable word on a "No Loitering" sign. Two or three girls joined us.

Tommy asked me about the trial, and I told him I was interested in helping teenagers, especially those in the gangs. The boys listened attentively, and several of them mentioned that I was "one of us."

"What do you mean, I'm one of you?" I asked.

Their logic was simple. The cops didn't like me; the cops didn't like them. We were in the same boat, and I was one of them. This was the first time, but by no means the last, that I heard this logic. I caught a glimpse of myself being hauled up that courtroom aisle, and it had a different light on it. I felt a shiver.

The boy with the knife stepped up to me. His words, although they were phrased in the language of the streets, cut my heart more surely than his knife would have been able to do.

"Davie," the boy said. He hiked his shoulders up to settle his jacket firmly on his back, and I noticed the other boys stepped back. Very deliberately, this boy closed and then opened his knife again. He held it out and casually ran the blade down the buttons of my coat, flicking them one by one without speaking.

"Davie," he said at last, looking me in the eye for the first time, "you're all right. But if you ever turn on boys in this town . . ." I felt the knifepoint press my belly lightly.

"What's your name, young man?" His name was Willie.

"Willie, I don't know why God brought me to this town.

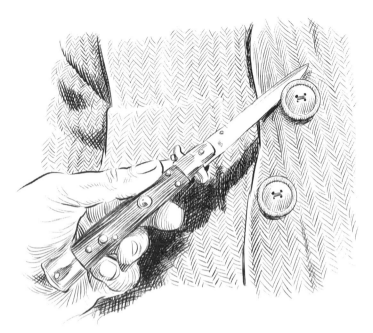

But let me tell you one thing. *He* is on your side. That I can promise you."

Willie's eyes hadn't left mine. But gradually I felt the pressure of the knifepoint lessen. Then his eyes broke away. He turned aside.

Tommy changed the subject. "Davie, if you want to meet the gangs, why don't you start right here? These guys are all Rebels, and I can show you some GGIs, too—Grand Gangsters, Incorporated."

I hadn't been in New York half an hour and already I was being introduced to my second street gang. Tommy called one of the girls standing nearby. "Nancy, take the preacher down to the GGIs, will you?"

The GGIs met in a basement on 134th Street. To reach their "clubroom" Nancy and I walked down a flight of cement stairs, weaving our way past garbage pails that were chained to the building and past a pile of vodka bottles. Finally Nancy stopped and rapped, two-quick, four-slow, on a door.

A girl opened it. She held a can of beer, and a cigarette hung sideways from her lips. Her hair was unkempt, and the shoulder of her dress was pulled down in a revealing way. This girl was a child, a girl in her teens.

"Maria?" said Nancy. "Can we come in? I want you to meet someone."

Maria shrugged and opened the door wider. The room inside was dark, and it took me a while to realize that it was filled with kids. Boys and girls of high school age sat together in this cold and ill-smelling room. Someone switched on a wan overhead lightbulb. The kids slowly looked up.

"This is that preacher that was kicked out of the Farmer trial," said Nancy.

Immediately, I had their attention—and their sympathy. That afternoon I had a chance to preach my first sermon to a New York gang. I didn't try to get a complicated message over to them, just that they were loved as they were, there, amid the vodka bottles and the boredom. God understood what they were looking for. And God had higher hopes for them.

Once, when I paused, a boy said, "Keep it up, Preach. You're coming through."

It was the first time I heard the expression. It was the highest compliment they could have paid my preaching.

I would have left that basement hideout, half an hour later, with a feeling of great encouragement, except for one thing. There, among the GGIs, I had my first encounter with narcotics. Maria—she turned out to be president of the GGI Debs, the girl-gang attached to the GGIs—interrupted me when I said that God could help them toward a new life.

"Not me, Davie."

"Why not you, Maria?"

She pulled up her sleeve and showed me her inner arm at the elbow. I could see little wounds on it like festered mosquito bites. Some were old and blue. Some were fresh. I suddenly knew what this teenage girl was trying to say to me. She was an addict.

"I'm a mainliner, Davie. There's no hope for me, not even from God."

I looked around the room. No one was smiling.

Maria had expressed the opinion of the experts: There was virtually no hope for the "mainline" addict, the one who injects heroin directly into the bloodstream.

Maria was a mainliner.

4

When I got back to our car, still parked on Broadway, Miles seemed truly glad to see me. I told him about the two gangs I had met within an hour of setting foot in New York. Miles had the same thought I had.

"You realize, of course, that you'd never have had a chance with them if you hadn't been thrown out of court and got your picture taken?"

We drove downtown, and this time we went in person to the DA's office.

"I wish there were some way," I said, "to convince you that I have no other motive than those boys' welfare in asking to see them."

"Reverend, if every word you're saying came straight from that Bible of yours, we still couldn't let you see them. The only way you can see those boys without Judge Davidson's permission is to get signed permission from each of the parents."

Here was another avenue opened up!

"Could you give me their names and addresses?"

"I'm sorry. That we would not be at liberty to do."

Back on the street I pulled the now tattered page from *Life* out of my pocket. Here was the name of the leader of the gang: Luis Alvarez. While Miles stayed with the car, I went into a candy store and changed a five-dollar bill—it was almost our last money—into dimes for the phone booth. Then I started to call all the Alvarezes in the telephone book.

"Is this the residence of Luis Alvarez, the one who is in the Michael Farmer trial?" I would ask.

An offended silence. Angry words. A receiver slammed in my ear. It became clear we would never reach our boys this way.

I joined Miles in the car. There in the car, with the skyscrapers of lower Manhattan towering over us, I bowed my head. "Lord," I prayed, "if we are here on Your errand, You must guide us. Lead where we must go, for we do not know."

We started to drive aimlessly in the direction the car was headed, which happened to be north. We got caught in a traffic jam at Times Square. When we extricated ourselves from that, it was only to get lost in Central Park. We drove round and round before we realized that the roads there form a circle. We took an exit just to be out of the park. We found ourselves on an avenue that led to the heart of Spanish Harlem. Suddenly, I had that same incomprehensible urge to get out of the car.

"Let's look for a parking place," I said to Miles.

We pulled into the first empty space we found. I got out of the car and took a few steps up the street. I stopped. The inner urging had gone away. A group of boys were sitting on a stoop.

"Where does Luis Alvarez live?" I asked one of them.

The boys stared at me and did not answer. I walked on.

A boy came running up the sidewalk after me. "You looking for Luis Alvarez?"

"Yes. Do you know him?"

The boy stared at me. "Is that your car?" he said.

"Yes. Why?"

The boy shrugged. "Man," he said, "you parked right in front of his house."

I felt bumps form on my flesh. I pointed at the tenement house in front of where I had parked. "He lives there?" I asked.

The boy nodded.

I have questioned God sometimes when prayers have gone unanswered. But answered prayer is still harder to believe. We asked God to guide us, and He set us down on Luis Alvarez's doorstep.

The name *Alvarez* was on the mailbox in the dingy vestibule—third floor. I raced up the stairs. The third-floor hall was dark and smelled of urine.

"Mr. Alvarez?" I called, finding a door with the name painted in neat letters.

Someone called out in Spanish from the interior of the apartment, and hoping it was an invitation to come in, I pushed the door open. I peered in. Seated in a red overstuffed chair was a slender man, dark-skinned, holding a rosary. When he saw me, his face lit up.

"You Davie," he spoke very slowly. "You are the preacher. The cops, they throw you out."

"Yes," I said. I walked in. Mr. Alvarez stood.

"I pray that you come," he said. "You will help my boy?"

"I want to, Mr. Alvarez. But they won't let me see Luis. I have to have written permission from you and from the other parents."

"I give that." Señor Alvarez got out a pencil and paper from the kitchen drawer. Slowly he wrote that I had his permission to see Luis Alvarez. Then he folded the paper and handed it to me.

"Do you have the names and addresses of the other boys' parents?"

"No," said Luis's father, and he shook his head slightly. "I don't keep so close touch on my son. God, He brought you here, He will bring you to the others."

So a few minutes after we had parked at random on a Spanish Harlem street, I had my first signed permission.

On my way down the dark stairs, I nearly collided with a boy, about seventeen, who was running full tilt up the stairs.

"Excuse me," I said, without stopping.

The boy looked at me. As I passed beneath an overhanging light, he looked at me again.

"Preacher?"

I turned.

"Aren't you the guy who was thrown out of Luis's trial?"

"I'm David Wilkerson, yes."

The boy thrust out his hand. "I'm Angelo Morales. I'm in Luis's gang. You been up to see the Alvarezes?"

"Yes." I told Angelo that I needed their permission in order to see Luis. "I have to get permission from *each* boy's parents. Mr. Alvarez didn't know where the other boys live. But you do, don't you?"

Angelo drove all over Spanish Harlem with us, locating the families of the six other defendants in the Michael Farmer trial. As we drove, Angelo told us about himself: He would have been with the boys that night they "messed Michael up," except that he had a toothache. He said the boys had not gone out with any particular plan in mind: They had just gone "rumbling" (looking for trouble). "If it hadn't been Farmer, they'd of been jitterbugging."

Jitterbugging meant gang fighting. Miles and I learned a lot from Angelo. The boys in this particular gang—were they all like this?—were bored, lonely and smolderingly angry. They craved excitement, and they took it where they could find it.

Angelo had an amazing way of making things clear. He was a bright, appealing boy, and he wanted to help. Miles and I agreed that no matter what happened, we would keep in touch with Angelo Morales. We would show him another way.

Within two hours we had every signature.

After we wrote down Angelo's address and promised to keep in touch, Miles and I drove back downtown, our hearts singing.

The district attorney was very surprised at seeing us again so soon. When we produced the required signatures, he called the jail and said that if the boys would see us, we must be allowed in.

But at the jail itself, a strange and totally unexpected block was thrown in our way. The prison chaplain who had the boys in his care considered that it would be "disturbing" to their spiritual welfare to introduce a new personality. Each of the boys had signed a form saying, "We will talk with Reverend David Wilkerson." The chaplain struck out the "will," and wrote in "will not." No amount of pleading persuaded the city that his decision should be overruled.

Once again, we headed back across the George Washington Bridge—very puzzled. Why was it that we had received such dramatic encouragement only to have the road end again at a blank wall?

As we drove along the Pennsylvania Turnpike late that night, I saw a ray of hope in the darkness around me in the form of a remarkable man: my father's father. I decided to pay him a visit, to place my puzzlement before him.

5

At home, I phoned Grandpap to say I wanted to see him.

"You come right on, son," he said. "We'll have us a talk."

My grandfather was 79 years old and as full of vinegar as ever. He himself was the son and the grandson, and perhaps the great-grandson, of a preacher. By the time Grandpap reached his twenties he was already a preacher. He was a circuit rider, which meant he spent a good part of his ministry in the saddle. He'd ride his horse from one small church to another.

Grandpap developed what he called "The Lamb Chop School" of evangelizing. "You win over people just like you win over a dog," he used to say. "You see a dog passing down the street with a bone in his mouth. You don't grab the bone from him. He'll growl at you. It's all he has. But you throw a big fat lamb chop in front of him, and he's going to drop that bone and pick up the lamb chop, his tail wagging to beat the band. Now you've got a friend. Instead of going around grabbing bones from people, I'm going to throw them some lamb chops. Something with real meat and life in it. I'm going to tell them about new beginnings."

My father was different. He was a minister more than an evangelist. My father built solid churches where he was beloved and sought out in times of trouble.

"It takes both kinds of preachers to make a church," my father said to me when I was a kid. "But I envy your grandfather's ability to shake the pride out of people."

Dad's church was in a fashionable suburb of Pittsburgh, among the bankers and lawyers and doctors of the city. It was an unusual setting for a church. Our services could be noisy and undignified, but we'd toned them down due to our surroundings. It took my grandfather to show us we were wrong.

One time Grandpap was passing through, and Dad asked him to preach a sermon the following Sunday night. I was at that service, and I'll never forget the look on Dad's face when the first thing Grandpap did was to take off his shoes and place them right smack in the middle of the altar rail!

"Now!" said Grandpap, staring out over the startled congregation. "What is it that bothers you about dirty shoes on the altar rail? I've smudged your beautiful little church with some dirt. I've hurt your pride, and I'll bet if I'd asked you the question, you'd say you don't have any pride."

Dad cringed.

"Go ahead and wriggle," Grandpap said, turning to him. "You need this, too. Where's all the deacons in this church?"

The deacons raised their hands.

"I want you to go around and open all the windows. We're getting ready to make some noise, and I want those bankers

and lawyers sitting on their porches on a Sunday night to hear what it's like to be glad in your religion."

Then Grandpap said he wanted everybody to start marching around the church clapping our hands. We marched and we clapped. He had us clap for fifteen minutes, and when we tried to quit he shook his head and we clapped some more. Then he started us singing. Now we were marching and clapping and singing, and every time we slowed down a little, Grandpap shoved open the windows another inch.

That was quite a service.

The next day Dad went to the bank on business and, sure enough, sitting behind a big desk was one of our neighbors. The banker called to him: "Say, Reverend Wilkerson. That was some singing at your church last night. Everyone's talking about it. We heard that you people could sing, and all this while we've been waiting to hear you. It's the best thing that ever happened in this neighborhood."

Grandpap was a praying man. Once he asked me, "David, do you dare to pray for help when you're in trouble?"

It seemed a peculiar question at first. I thanked God often for the good things that came my way, certainly, like parents and home, or food and schooling. I prayed that the Lord would some day in some way choose to work through me. But to pray for specific help, that I rarely did.

"David," said Grandpap, "the day you learn to be publicly specific in your prayers, *that* is the day you will discover power."

I didn't quite understand what he meant, partly because I was just twelve years old, and partly because I was afraid of the idea. It meant saying, in the hearing of others, "I ask for such and such," and taking the risk that the prayer would not be answered.

By accident I was forced, one dreadful day, to discover what Grandpap meant. During all of my childhood, my father had been a very sick man. He had duodenal ulcers, and for more than ten years he had been in pain.

One day, walking home from school, I saw an ambulance tear past. When I was still more than a block away from home, I knew where it had been heading. From that distance I could hear my father's screams.

A group of elders from the church sat solemnly in the living room. The doctor wouldn't let me in the room where Dad was, so Mother joined me in the hall.

"Is he going to die, Mom?"

Mother looked me in the eye and decided to tell the truth. "The doctor thinks he may live two more hours."

Just then Dad gave a loud cry of pain, and Mother ran back into the room. Before the door closed, I saw why the doctor wouldn't allow me in Dad's room. The bedsheets and floor were drenched with blood.

At that moment I remembered my Grandfather's promise: "The day you learn to be publicly specific in your prayers is the day you will discover power." For a moment I thought of walking in to where the men sat in the living room and announcing that I was praying for my father to get up from his bed a healed man. I couldn't do it.

Instead, I ran down the basement stairs, and there I prayed, trying to substitute volume of voice for the belief that I lacked.

What I didn't realize was that I was praying into a kind of loudspeaker system.

Our house was heated by hot air, and the great trumpet-like pipes branched out from the basement furnace into every room of the house. My voice carried up those pipes so that the men from the church, sitting in the living room, heard a fervent voice pouring out of the walls. The doctor heard it. My father, lying on his deathbed, heard it.

"Bring David here," he whispered.

I was brought upstairs past the staring eyes of the elders and into my father's room. Dad asked Dr. Brown to wait in the hall for a moment, then he told Mother to read aloud the 22nd verse of the 21st chapter of Matthew. Mother opened the Bible. "And all things, whatsoever ye shall ask in prayer," she read, "believing, ye shall receive."

While my father lay limp on his bed, Mother read the same passage over and over again, a dozen or so times. I felt a tremendous excitement. I walked over to Dad's bed and laid my hands on his forehead.

"Jesus," I prayed, "I believe what You said. Make Daddy well!"

There was one more step. I walked to the door and opened it and said, loud and clear: "Please come, Dr. Brown. I have—" it was hard to say—"I have prayed believing that Daddy will get better."

Dr. Brown looked down at my twelve-year-old earnest-ness and smiled a warm and totally unbelieving smile. But that smile turned to astonishment as he bent to examine my father.

"Something has happened," he said. His voice was so low I could hardly hear. Dr. Brown tested Dad's blood pressure. "Kenneth," he said, feeling Dad's abdomen and then reading his blood pressure again. "Kenneth, how do you feel?"

"Like strength is flowing into me."

"Kenneth," said the doctor, "I have just witnessed a miracle."

My father was able to get up from his bed in that miraculous moment. In that same moment I was delivered of any doubts about the power of getting out on a limb in prayer.

Driving down to Grandfather's farm so many years later, this was one of the memories I brought with me.

I was glad to see Grandpap was as alert as ever. He was a little slower in his movements, but quick of mind. He sat in a straight chair, straddling it backward, and listened as I told him about my strange experiences. He let me talk for an hour, interrupting only to ask questions.

"What do you make of it, Grandpap? Do you think I had a real call to help the boys in the murder trial?"

"No, I don't," said Grandpap. "I think that door's slammed just about as tight as you'll ever find a door shut, David. I don't think the Lord's going to let you see those seven boys for a long time. I'll tell you why. Because if you see them now, you may figure you've done your duty among the teenage boys in New York. I think there are *bigger* plans for you."

"How do you mean?"

"I've got a feeling, son, that you were never intended to see just seven boys, but thousands of boys just like them."

Grandpap let that sink in. Then he went on.

"I mean all the mixed-up boys of New York who might end up murdering for kicks unless you help them. I have a feeling that the only thing you need do is expand your horizons."

My grandfather had a way of putting things that left me inspired. From wanting to get away from the city as fast as possible, I suddenly found myself wanting to rush right back and get to work. I said something like this to Grandpap, and he smiled.

"That's easy to say, sitting here in this warm kitchen talking to your old grandfather. But wait until you meet more of these boys before you start having visions. They'll be full of hate and sin, worse than you've even heard of. They're just boys, but they know what evil is. And Davie, you've got to keep your eye focused on the central heart of the Gospel. What would you say that is?"

I looked him in the eye. "I've heard my own grandfather often enough on this subject," I said, "to give him an answer from his own sermons. The heart of the Gospel is change. It is being born again to a new life."

"You rattle that off pretty smooth, David. But that's the heart of Christ's message. An encounter with God—a real one—means change."

Grandpap unfolded himself stiffly from his chair and started walking toward the farmhouse door.

"Davie," said Grandpap, "I'm still worried about you when you meet the raw life of the city. You've been sheltered. When you meet wickedness in the flesh, it could petrify you.

"You know . . . some time ago I was taking a walk through the hills when I came across an enormous snake. He was a big one, Davie, three inches thick and four feet long, and he just lay there in the sun looking scary. I was afraid of this thing, and I didn't move for a long time. But lo and behold, while I was watching, I saw that old snake shed its skin and leave it lying there in the sun and go off a new creature.

"When you start your new work in the city, don't you

be like I was, petrified by the outward appearance of your boys. God isn't. He's just waiting for each one of them to crawl right out of that old sin-shell and leave it behind. He's waiting and yearning for the new man to come out.

"Never forget that, David, when you see your snakes, as surely you will, on the sidewalks of New York."

6

When I drove to New York next, I was no longer a man with the simple mission of helping seven boys. There was a new vision, and I only knew that it had to do with specific help I was supposed to give boys like Luis and his friends.

"Lord," I said, "if You have work for me in this place, teach me what it is."

This was the beginning of a four-month-long walk through the streets of New York. During the months of March, April, May, and June of 1958, I drove to the city every week, using my day off for the trip. I would rise early and make the eight-hour drive, arriving in New York in the early afternoon. Then, until deep into the night, I roamed the streets, driving home in early morning.

These were not idle explorations. The feeling of being guided by a purpose other than my own never left me, though the nature of it was more mysterious than ever. I knew of no other way to respond than to return to the city again and again, holding myself open, always waiting for the direction to become clear.

I remember the first night of this four-month walk. Maria had told me that one of the roughest, most brutal neighborhoods in all New York was the Bedford-Stuyvesant section of Brooklyn.

"Preacher," said Maria, "if you want to see New York at its worst, you just drive across the Brooklyn Bridge and open your eyes."

So I drove for the first time into the heart of an area that at the time was supposed to have more murders per square foot of land than any place on earth.

It was a cold March night when I pulled into the area and parked my car. Across the street a group of teenagers were hanging around. They wore leather jackets with a curious insignia stenciled on the back. I wanted to talk to them, but I hesitated.

In the end I didn't cross the street—not that night. I just walked, past bars and overflowing garbage cans, past storefront churches and police stations and on into an immense housing project with broken windows and broken lights and a broken "Keep Off the Grass" sign on the ground.

On the way back to my car I heard what sounded to me like three quick shots. Then I thought I must have been mistaken, because no one on the street seemed excited. Within minutes a police car roared by, siren screaming, to pull into the curb with its light flashing red. Only a few people stopped to watch as they brought a man out of a building, dripping blood.

I went back to my car, and after hanging an old shirt in

the window for some privacy, I lay down, pulled a rug over me, and went to sleep.

I wouldn't do that today. I know better. But in the morning I woke up safe. Was it the words from the 91st Psalm that I said as I fell asleep that kept me safe?

Because thou hast made the LORD, which is my refuge, even the most High, thy habitation; there shall no evil befall thee, neither shall any plague come nigh thy dwelling. For he shall give his angels charge over thee, to keep thee in all thy ways. They shall bear thee up in their hands, lest thou dash thy foot against a stone. Thou shalt tread upon the lion and adder: the young lion and the dragon shalt thou trample under feet.

Bit by bit, during this four-month walk, I got to know the streets. Angelo was very helpful in this. (I had kept in close touch with him.)

One day as Angelo and I walked down a street together, I asked him, "What would you say was the greatest problem boys have in this city?"

"Lonesomeness," said Angelo.

It was a strange answer; lonesomeness in a city of eight million people. But Angelo said the feeling came because nobody loved you. All of his friends in gangs were lonely. The more I came to know New York, the more I realized that Angelo was right.

These boys were never far from violence. I know of one instance when a fight took two months to plan; but I know of another case when at two o'clock in the afternoon ten boys were standing around a street corner drinking pop, and at four o'clock that same afternoon one of the boys was dead, two others in the hospital: A major war between rival gangs had flared up, raged and ended in the interval.

I reached the point where I could spot peddlers of drugs. They were bold and pushy. They talked freely about their trade.

Once, during my long walk, I heard a high, piercing scream. No one paid the slightest attention. The screaming went on and on.

"That sounds like someone in pain," I said to a woman who was resting her arms on a first-floor windowsill in the same building.

She lifted her head, listened a minute, and shrugged her shoulders.

"Third floor," she said. "It's terrible. He's twenty years old. It's heroin. He's really hooked and can't get a fix."

"You know who he is?"

"Since he was in diapers."

"Can't we take him to a hospital?"

The woman looked at me. "Mister," she said, "you're new here, aren't you?"

"Yes."

"You try to get a hooked boy into one of these hospitals and see where you get."

How those words would come back to me in the months to come.

Fighting and drug addiction: These were dramatic manifestations of the needs of New York's teenage gang members. But as Angelo said, they were just the outward symbols of a deep inner need: loneliness. A hunger for some kind of significance. I found on this long walk how pathetically low these boys' sights were. They were pitifully isolated, each in his own small turf. I met dozens of Brooklyn youngsters who had never been across the Brooklyn Bridge for fear of enemy gangs in Manhattan and the Bronx.

A pattern emerged. It was a pattern of need, starting with loneliness and extending through the gang wars, the wild parties, the addiction, and ending in an early grave.

To check my own impressions, I visited police stations, talked with social workers and parole officers, and spent many hours in the library. In the end, my total impression of the problems of New York teenagers was so staggering that I almost quit. That was when the Holy Spirit stepped in to help.

This time, He did not come to my aid in any dramatic way; He simply gave me an idea.

I was driving back to Philipsburg, and I asked myself, "Suppose you were to be granted a wish for these kids. What would be the one best thing you could hope for?"

I knew my answer: that they could begin life all over again, with the innocent personalities of newborn children. And that this time as they were growing up they could be surrounded by love instead of by hate and fear.

They've got to start over again, and they've got to be surrounded by love.

The idea came to mind as a complete thought, as clearly as the first order to go to New York. Along with it came into my mind the picture of a house where these kids could come. A really nice house, where they would be welcomed—and loved. They could live in their house any time they wanted to. The door would always be open; there would be lots of beds, and clothes to wear, and a great big kitchen.

"Oh, Lord," I said aloud, "what a wonderful dream! But it would take a series of miracles such as I've never seen."

7

I made my next trip to New York a week later, in a strange state of mind. In part I was elated by my new dream, and in part I was confused.

The enemy lurked in the conditions that made up the slums of New York, ready to grab lonesome and love-starved boys. He held out easy promises of security and freedom, of happiness and of retribution. Against his strength, I considered my own weakness. I had none of the usual weapons. I had no experience. I had no money. I had no organization backing me. I was afraid of the fight.

I found myself remembering another occasion when I'd seen a fight coming and had been afraid. It happened when I was a boy, and we had just moved to Pittsburgh. I was always skinny. The very idea of a fistfight left me shaking.

Still, the funny thing is that, all through my high school years, I never had to fight because I had a reputation for being tough. That ridiculous situation came about in a peculiar way, and the more I thought about it, the more I wondered if it might have significance for me now.

There was a boy in school named Chuck who was a bully. I learned he always beat up the new kids, and he was especially tough on preachers' kids.

Chuck had me shaking before I ever saw him. What was I going to do when we finally did meet? I asked God this question and an answer came quickly and clearly: *Not by might, nor by power, but by my spirit.* I knew it was a Bible quotation—Zechariah 4:6—and then and there I took it for my motto. When the time came to face Chuck, I would lean on this promise; God would give me a boldness that would be equal to any bully.

One afternoon I started home from school. Suddenly, I saw a boy walking toward me. I knew in an instant this was Chuck. He was strutting down the opposite side of the street. But when he saw me he crossed over and bore down on me like an angry bull.

Chuck stopped dead in my path. He must have weighed fifty pounds more than I, and he towered above me so that I had to bend my neck to look him in the eye.

"You're the preacher's kid."

I was scared to the core.

Not by might, nor by power, but by my spirit. Not by might, nor by power, but by my spirit, saith the LORD of hosts. I kept repeating this sentence over and over to myself while Chuck commenced to give his opinion of me. First he picked on the fact that I looked stupid. Then he worked over the obvious truth that I was a weakling. After that he had a few words to say about preachers' kids in general.

By my spirit, saith the LORD. I still had not spoken, but inside me an amazing event was taking place. I felt fear melting, and in its place came confidence and joy. I looked up at Chuck and smiled.

Chuck was getting mad. His face turned red as he challenged me to fight.

Still I smiled.

Chuck started to circle me with his fists clenched. In his face, though, I saw a hint of alarm.

I circled, too, never taking my eyes off his, and all the while I smiled.

Finally, Chuck hit me. It was a hesitant little blow that didn't hurt, and it happened to catch me on balance so I wasn't thrown. I laughed, low and secretly.

Chuck stopped circling. He dropped his fists. Then he turned and took off down the street.

Next day at school, I began to hear how I'd beaten up the biggest bully in town. Chuck had been telling everyone. He said I was the toughest guy he ever fought. Apparently he laid it on thick, because after that I was treated with respect by the entire school. Perhaps I should have told the kids the truth, but I never did. I had a kind of insurance policy in my reputation. And, hating to fight as I did, I wasn't about ready to turn my policy in.

Now I wondered—wasn't I facing the same problem, an enemy far bigger and more powerful than I? I knew absolutely that I could not depend upon myself. If I were right in dreaming about a new beginning and a new environment for these boys and girls, perhaps God would choose just such an ill-equipped person as I, so that the work from the very start would depend on Him alone. "Not by might, nor by power, but by my spirit, saith the LORD of hosts."

I decided to take a first step toward making my dream

come true. The very first thing I needed to know was whether I had any right to be glimpsing such visions. Was it really possible for teenage New York gang members to change in the radical way I was dreaming about? I remembered how Grandfather insisted that at the heart of the Gospel message was a transforming experience. I knew by memory the passage in John 3 that he was referring to. "Verily, verily, I say unto thee, Except a man be born again, he cannot see the kingdom of God."

If these boys were going to change dramatically, the transformation would have to come about in their hearts. I knew *I* could never bring this about: It would have to be the work of the Holy Spirit. But perhaps I could act as a channel through which the Spirit would reach these boys.

I started making inquiries: What were the toughest, hardest gangs in town? Time and again two names recurred—the Chaplains and the Mau Maus. Both were in Fort Greene, Brooklyn.

These gangs had their turfs in one of the world's largest housing developments: Fort Greene Projects. More than thirty thousand people lived in these towering apartments, a heavy percentage of them on welfare.

The Chaplains were African Americans; the Mau Maus, Spanish. The two gangs did not fight each other, but joined together to protect their turf against outside gangs. I decided Fort Greene would be the testing ground.

One Friday morning I picked up a friend of mine, a trumpet player named Jimmy Stahl, and the two of us drove over the Brooklyn Bridge and into the Fort Greene Housing Project. We parked our car.

"You stand here near this lamppost," I told Jimmy, "and

start blowing. If we get a crowd, I'll step up on the base of the post and talk to them."

Jimmy began to play "Onward Christian Soldiers" on his trumpet. He played it over and over, lively and loud.

Windows flew open and heads popped out. Children began to swarm out of the buildings. Next, the teenagers began to arrive. Everyone wore sunglasses.

After Jimmy played his piece fifteen or twenty times, around a hundred boys and girls had gathered. They milled about shouting to each other and to us, obscenities mingled with the catcalls. I climbed up on the lamp base and began to talk. The uproar increased. I didn't know what to do next. Jimmy shook his head. "They can't hear you!" he formed with his lips.

At that moment the problem was taken out of my hands. I saw a police car pull to the curb. Officers stepped out and started working their way through the crowd, poking with their nightsticks.

"All right. Break it up."

The youngsters parted to let the police through but closed ranks again behind them.

"Get down from there," one of the officers said to me. "What are you trying to do, start a riot?"

"I'm preaching."

"Well, you're not preaching here. We've got enough trouble in this neighborhood without having a mob on our hands."

Now the boys and girls began shouting that the police couldn't stop me from preaching. It was against the Constitution, they said. But before Jimmy and I knew what was happening, we were being shoved bodily through the crowd toward the police car.

At the station house, I picked up the theme the kids had used. "Let me ask you something," I said. "Isn't it my right as a citizen to speak on a public street?"

"You can," admitted the police, "as long as you speak under an American flag."

Half an hour later Jimmy started to blow "Onward Christian Soldiers" again. This time we had an enormous American flag floating behind us, borrowed from the sympathetic principal of a nearby school. And this time, instead of preaching from a lamppost base, I had a piano stool to stand on.

Again windows flew open, and small children swarmed around us. And again we were faced, a few minutes later, with a hooting, catcalling teenage mob. Only now we were heroes, because we had been taken in by the police.

Our new popularity, though, did not improve the manners of our audience. I stood on my stool and tried to raise my voice above the din. But nobody was listening. Directly in front of me a boy and girl were doing a grinding dance that brought whistles and clapping from onlookers. Others picked up dancing themselves, cigarettes hanging sideways from their mouths.

In despair, I bowed my head. *Lord, if You are doing a work here, I will have to ask You even for their attention.*

While I was still praying, the change began.

It was the children who settled down first. But when I opened my eyes I noticed that a lot of the older boys who had been leaning up against the school fence, smoking, had straightened up and were now standing with heads slightly bowed.

I was so startled by the sudden silence that I was at a loss for words.

Finally I began to speak. I chose John 3:16 as my text: "For God so loved the world, that he gave his only begotten Son, that whosoever believeth in him should not perish, but have everlasting life." I told them God loved them as they were, right then. He knew what they were. He knew their hatred and their anger. He knew that some of them had committed murder. But God also saw what they were going to be in the future, not only what they had been in the past.

That was all. I had said what I had to say, and I stopped.

A silence hung over the street. I could hear the flag flapping in the breeze. I told the kids then that I was going to ask for something special to happen to them. I was going to ask that their lives be completely changed in the next moment.

I bowed my head again and prayed. I raised my head and asked if anyone wanted to come up front where we could talk. No response.

Suddenly I heard myself saying, without any intention on my part, "All right, now. They tell me that you've got a couple of pretty tough gangs here in Fort Greene. I want to talk to your presidents and your vice presidents. If you are so tough, you won't mind coming up and shaking hands with a skinny preacher."

For a minute, nobody stirred. Then someone called, "What's the matter, Buckboard? You scared?"

Slowly a big African-American kid left his station at the rear of the crowd and came forward. A second boy followed. On their way through the crowd they picked up two more boys and all four grouped themselves in front of me.

The big one stepped forward another few inches.

"Slip me some skin, Preacher," he said. "I'm Buckboard, president of the Chaplains."

I was still innocent of the slang of New York, and when he held out his hand I tried to grasp it. "Just slip it, Preach," and he slid his open palm along mine. He stood for a minute, examining me curiously. "You're all right, Preacher. You really bugged me."

Buckboard then introduced me to his vice president, Stagecoach, and to his two warlords.

What was I going to do now? With my heart pounding, I nodded to Jimmy, and we walked the four boys a few yards away from the crowd. Stagecoach kept saying our message was "coming through."

I told the four boys it wasn't I who was coming through but the Holy Spirit, trying to reach them. "The Holy Spirit

wants to get inside that shell and help you start all over again."

"What we supposed to do, man?"

In a church I might have asked these boys to come forward and kneel at the altar. But how could you ask them to do that on a street in front of friends?

Or maybe such a bold step was needed. The change in their lives we were asking for was drastic, so maybe the symbol had to be drastic, too.

"What are you supposed to do?" I said. "I want you to kneel down right here on the street and ask the Holy Spirit to come into your lives so that you will become new men. 'New creatures in Christ' is what the Bible says: This can happen to you, too."

There was a long pause. I was aware of the crowd waiting, very quietly, to see what was going to happen. Finally Stagecoach said, in a hoarse voice, "Buckboard? You want to? I will if you will."

Before my astonished eyes, these two leaders of one of the most feared fighting gangs in all of New York slowly dropped to their knees. Their warlords followed their lead.

"Lord Jesus," I said, "here are four of Your own children, doing something that is very hard. They are kneeling here before everyone and asking You to come into their hearts and make them new. They want You to take away the hate, and the fighting, and the loneliness. They want to *know* for the first time in their lives that they are really loved. They are asking this of You, Lord, and You will not disappoint them. Amen."

Buckboard and Stagecoach got up. The two warlords followed. They did not lift their heads. I suggested they might want to get off by themselves for a while, maybe find a church somewhere.

Without speaking, the boys turned and made their way through the crowd. Someone called out, "Hey, Buckboard! What's it like when you got religion?"

Buckboard told them to lay off, and he was taunted no more.

Jimmy and I left Fort Greene with our heads swimming. We had not expected God to answer us in such a dramatic manner. Buckboard, Stagecoach, and two warlords falling to their knees on a street corner: It was almost too much to believe.

Frankly, we'd been better prepared for the reaction of the Mau Mau leaders. They were in the crowd, watching Buckboard and Stagecoach with mingled contempt and fascination. After the Chaplains had departed, the crowd began to call for them.

"Israel! Nicky! You're next! Come on. You going to chicken out?" Such shouts urged them forward.

Israel, the president of the gang, was as nice a boy as I've met: He stuck out his hand and shook mine like a gentleman.

Nicky was something else. I remember thinking, as I looked at him, *That's the hardest face I have ever seen.*

"How do you do, Nicky," I said.

He left me standing with my hand outstretched. He wouldn't even look at me. He puffed on a cigarette, shooting nervous jets of smoke out the side of his mouth.

"Go to hell, Preacher," he said. He had an odd, strangled way of speaking, and he stuttered.

"You don't think much of me, Nicky," I said, "but I feel different about you. I love you." I took a step toward him.

"You come near me, Preacher," he said in that tortured voice, "I'll kill you."

"You could do that," I agreed. "You could cut me in a thousand pieces and lay them out in the street and every piece would love you." But as I said it, I was thinking, *And it wouldn't do a bit of good—not with you, Nicky. There's no love on earth that could reach you.*

Before we left Brooklyn, we put Buckboard and Stagecoach in touch with a local minister. "I think," I said to Jimmy, "we'd better check in on them from time to time, too." To be perfectly honest, neither one of us could rid himself of the suspicion that the boys were having some fun with us.

When I later told Gwen that, she scolded me.

"David Wilkerson," she said, "don't you realize that you got exactly what you wanted? You asked the Holy Spirit for a miracle, and now that you've got one you're trying to argue it away. People who don't believe in miracles shouldn't pray for them."

8

It seemed to me that I had passed the first milestone on the road toward my dream. I had been given hope. I even dared to hope that perhaps I would be allowed at last to see Luis. I heard from Angelo that Luis was supposed to be transferred to the Elmira, New York, prison.

"Do you think I could get to see him?" I asked.

"Not a chance, Davie. Once they learned you were the preacher at the trial, they'd never let you in."

Still, I wanted to try. I made inquiries and was told to write a letter, stating my relationship with the prisoner and why I wanted to see him. The request would be considered.

So that was that: I'd have to tell the truth, and I'd never be allowed in. But I did hear which day some boys were being transferred to Elmira. I went down to the train station and waited. When the train came in, about twenty boys were marched off. I scanned each of their faces, but Luis was not among them.

But if the Holy Spirit was closing that door to me, He was opening others. One warm night in early spring 1958,

I was walking through a busy, noisy street in Spanish Harlem when I heard singing. I was surprised to recognize the tune as a gospel song, being sung in Spanish. There was no church nearby; the music seemed to come from a window in one of the walk-up tenements I was passing.

"Who is that singing?" I asked a young man who was sitting on the fender of an automobile, smoking a cigarette.

The boy cocked his head to listen.

"That's some kind of church," he said. "Upstairs. Second floor."

I walked up the stairs and knocked on a door. It opened slowly, but when the light hit my face, the woman standing inside gave a little shriek. In her excitement she half-closed the door on me, and turned around rattling off something in Spanish. Soon the doorway was filled with smiling, friendly people. They took me by the arm and pulled me into the apartment.

"You are David!" one man said. "Aren't you the preacher who was thrown out of court?"

It turned out that this was what is known as an out-station church in the Spanish branch of the Assemblies of God. The people of an out-station meet in private homes until they can afford to build. They had followed the Michael Farmer trial closely and had seen my picture.

"We have been praying for you, and now you are here," one man said. His name was Vincente Ortez, and he was the minister of the little church. "We want to hear how you came to be at the trial," he said.

So that night, I had a chance to tell this group of believers about the way God seemed to be leading me into New York's streets. I told them what I'd learned about the problems boys and girls faced with the gangs, and with drinks and narcotics. I told them about my dream and about the first milestone I had passed. "I think God put that idea into my head, 'They've got to begin again, and they've got to be surrounded with love,'" I said, summing up. "We've seen how the Holy Spirit can reach them right on the street."

I realized I was more excited about these young people than I had guessed. By the time I had finished, I could see that these good people felt my urgency at the need.

When I sat down, these men and women held a brief discussion. They spoke for a few minutes, and then pushed Reverend Ortez forward as spokesman.

"Do you think," he said, "that you could come back tomorrow to talk to us, when we could have some more ministers in to hear you?" I said that I could.

As quietly as that, a new ministry was born. Like most things born of the Spirit, it came simply, without fanfare. Certainly, none of us that night knew what had begun.

"What's your address here?" Reverend Ortez asked. "Where can we call you about the time and place?"

I had to admit that I had no address. I didn't have the money for a hotel room. "I am, in fact," I said, "sleeping in my car."

Real alarm came over Reverend Ortez's face. "You mustn't do that," he said, and everyone in the room agreed. "It's more dangerous than you know. You stay here in our house—this night and any night you are in town."

I accepted this kindness gratefully. Reverend Ortez introduced me to his wife, Delia. I was shown to a room with a bunk bed in it, and I have never slept better than I did that first night off the streets.

The next morning I spent in prayer. It was far more than coincidence that I had dropped into that home church. What was going to happen now, I could not imagine, but I wanted to be ready to step out in whatever direction the Holy Spirit should point.

While I was at prayer, Reverend Ortez and his wife were constantly on the telephone. By the time we arrived at the church where the meeting was to take place, representatives of 65 Spanish Assemblies were gathered to hear what I had to say.

This time I related the events that had brought me to the city. I told about the embarrassment of the trial and of the puzzling, gnawing feeling I'd had ever since, that behind these seeming mistakes was a purpose I had barely glimpsed.

"I'll tell you frankly that I don't know what I am supposed to do next. The experience at Fort Greene may have been a one-time thing. I have no idea that it could be repeated on a larger scale."

Before the meeting was over, those 65 churches had come forward with a plan of action that would determine whether or not Fort Greene had been a one-time experience. They would hold a mass rally for teenagers in St. Nicholas Arena, a prizefight center in New York, where I could address many gangs at once.

I was hesitant. In the first place, I wasn't sure that mass meetings were the right approach. And it would take thousands of dollars to rent a big arena.

A man jumped to his feet in the back of the church and shouted something. I finally made it out. "Davie," he was saying, "everything is going to be all right."

After the meeting, the man introduced himself. He was Benigno Delgado, an attorney. Once again he repeated his statement that everything was going to be all right.

"Davie, you go to St. Nicholas Arena," he said. "You rent it and talk to these kids. Everything will work out." Then Mr. Delgado pulled from his pocket the largest roll of bills I had ever seen. "You talk to those children, Davie. I will rent the arena." And he did.

This was how, literally overnight, I became involved in a citywide youth rally, scheduled to be held in St. Nicholas Arena during the second week of July 1958.

When I returned to Philipsburg with the news, everyone became excited.

Only Gwen was quiet. "You realize," she said, "that's when the baby's due."

I hadn't realized. I mumbled something or other about the baby coming late.

Gwen laughed. "It'll be right on time," she said, "and you'll have your head in the clouds somewhere and won't even know it, and one day I'll present you with a little bundle. I don't think you really know a child exists anyway until he walks up to you and says, 'Daddy.'"

Which was doubtless true.

The church in Philipsburg was most generous, not only with its money support during the next two months when I could give it so little of my attention, but with its enthusiasm. I'd been keeping everyone posted on my trips to the city, telling of the tremendous problems these young teens faced. So they knew how much a part they were of anything the Lord was planning for New York.

As July approached, I found myself spending more time in the Ortez apartment. The Spanish churches supplied us with street workers who posted bulletins all over New York announcing the weeklong meetings. They trained counselors to be available in the dressing rooms of the arena for boys and girls who might decide to try a new beginning. They arranged for music and ushers and they handled the practical arrangements with the arena.

All I had to do was supply the teenagers.

But the closer we came to zero hour, the more I doubted the wisdom of this big rally.

Walking the streets, I'd talked to hundreds of boys and girls, but I'd never, until now, grasped what it was like to be inside their desperation. The simple prospect of traveling a few miles and entering a large building, so routine to you and me, loomed for them as an immense and peril-filled undertaking. They were afraid in the first place to leave their own turfs, afraid that as they passed through another gang's territory, they would be jumped. They were afraid of large groups of people, afraid of their own hates and prejudices, afraid that their anger and insecurity would erupt out of control into bloody fighting.

Strangest of all, they were afraid that something in the rally might make them cry. Bit by bit I came to realize the horror these young people had of tears.

What is it about tears that should be so terrifying? I learned that tears to them were a sign of weakness in a harsh world where only the tough survive.

Yet I knew how important tears are in making a person

whole. When finally we let the Holy Spirit into our innermost sanctuary, the reaction is to cry. I have seen it happen again and again. Deep soul-shaking weeping. It comes when that last barrier is down and you surrender yourself to wholeness.

When it comes, it ushers forth such a new personality that, from the days of Christ on, the experience has been spoken of as a birth. "You must be born again," said Jesus. At the heart of this newborn personality is joy; yet the joy is ushered in by tears.

What instinct told these boys and girls they might have to cry if they came into contact with God? They had their own way of expressing this fear, of course. I paid return visits to the gangs I had met, the Rebels and the GGIs, the Chaplains and the Mau Maus, inviting them to the rally, and everywhere it was the same. "You're not going to bug me, Preacher. You're not going to get me bawling."

One night, some time after I had been to the basement hideout of the GGIs with the news of the rally, there was a knock on the door of the Ortez apartment. Delia Ortez looked at her husband with raised eyebrows; he shook his head: No, he wasn't expecting anyone. Delia put down a knife with which she had been slicing meat and walked to the door.

There stood Maria. As soon as she stepped into the room I knew that she was high on heroin. Her eyes shone with an unnatural brightness; her hair was all over her face; her hands shook at her side.

"Maria!" I said, getting up. "Come in."

Maria came into the center of the room and demanded to know why we were trying to break up her gang.

"How do you mean, Maria?" said Delia.

"Trying to get the kids to a church service. You want to break us up." Then Maria began to curse us roundly.

One of the Ortez children came into the room, and Delia moved instinctively to stand next to the child. In that moment Maria rushed to the table where Delia had laid the butcher knife. One sweeping movement and the knife was in her fist, its long blade flashing. Delia jumped quickly between Maria and the child. Vincente leapt to his feet and started across the room.

"Stand back!" yelled Maria. Vincente stopped, because the girl had lifted the knife to her own neck. "I'm going to cut my throat. I'm going to stick myself like a pig and you're going to watch."

All of us in that room knew enough about the despair of the addict to know this was serious. Delia started talking rapidly about the long and wonderful life Maria had ahead of her. "God needs you, Maria," said Delia over and over again.

Over a five-minute period, while Delia never stopped talking, Maria's knife slipped lower and lower until finally it hung from her hand down at her hip. Still talking, Delia inched closer and at last, with one beautiful and agile leap, she knocked the knife from Maria's hand. It clattered to the floor.

Maria simply stood in the center of the room, the most forlorn bundle of dejection I had ever encountered. Suddenly she began to moan. She hid her face in her hands. "There's no out for me," she said. "I'm hooked and there's no way out."

"Why don't you give God a chance with you?" I asked her.

"No. That's not for me."

"Well, at least let the other kids come. Think—maybe they can find the way out before it's too late."

Maria straightened up. She seemed to have gotten back her composure. She shrugged her shoulders. "It depends if you've got a good show," said Maria. With that, she turned and walked out of the Ortez apartment, head high and hips swinging.

9

had never appreciated how much went into mounting a show. We set up a system of special buses that would pick up each gang on its own turf and take it nonstop to the arena. Workers from the 65 sponsoring churches combed the streets, alerting gang members to the arrangements.

On the fourth night, a hundred people showed up. The arena could hold seven thousand.

I remember standing at a little window on the balcony, where I could watch the teenagers arrive without being seen myself. Each night I hoped for a breakthrough. Each night only a handful of people straggled off the special buses and made their way into the arena.

The teenagers who did come, came for a show. It was difficult talking to an empty auditorium with the youngsters blowing smoke rings in your face and making lewd remarks.

The worst of it was what the kids call "breaking up." Whenever they didn't understand something, or didn't believe it, they began to laugh. I got so I dreaded to go out on the platform for fear of that laughter. The fourth night was the worst I'd ever known it. I did my best to build the meeting to a certain pitch of dignity and solemnity, and then all of a sudden one of the ringleaders snickered. Someone else picked it up and, before I could stop it, the whole bunch of them were holding their sides with laughter.

I cut the meeting short that night and went home ready to quit.

"Lord," I said, "we're not even beginning to reach these kids. What am I supposed to do?"

As always—why is it I had to learn this again every time?—when I really asked, I was really answered.

I met Jo-Jo the next day in Brooklyn. Jo-Jo was pointed out to me as the president of the Coney Island Dragons, one of the largest street gangs in the city. I walked up to this boy and stuck out my hand.

Jo-Jo's first act was to slap me across the palm. Then he leaned over and spit on my shoes. In the gangs this is the highest sign of contempt. He walked away and sat down on a bench with his back to me.

I walked over and sat beside him. I said, "Jo-Jo, where do you live?"

"Preacher, I don't want to talk to you. I don't want to have anything to do with you."

"But I want to have something to do with you," I said. "I'm going to stay here until I find out where you live."

"Preacher," said Jo-Jo, "you're sitting in my parlor."

"Where do you go when it rains?"

He said, "I move down to my suite in the subway."

Jo-Jo had on a pair of old canvas shoes. His toe was sticking out on the right foot, and he had a dirty black shirt on and a too-big pair of khaki trousers. He looked down at my brand-new shoes.

Jo-Jo said, "Look, rich man, it's all right for you to come here to New York and talk big about God changing lives. You've got new shoes and you've got good clothes. Look at me! I'm a bum. There are ten kids in my family. My people kicked me out—there wasn't enough food to go around."

I took off my shoes and asked him to try them on.

"What are you trying to prove? I'm not going to put your stinking shoes on."

"You've been griping about shoes. Put them on."

Jo-Jo put on the shoes. They fit.

Then I got up and walked away. I walked down the street in my stocking feet, about two blocks, to the car. Jo-Jo came up behind me and said, "You forgot your shoes."

"They're your shoes." I got in the car.

"Preacher," Jo-Jo said, reaching inside the window, "I forgot to shake your hand."

So we shook. Then I said, "Look. You don't have any place to live. I'm bumming a bed myself right now. But there's a couch out in the living room. Maybe the folks who took me in will take you in, too. Let's go ask them."

"Okay," said Jo-Jo, just like that. He got in the car, and we drove to the apartment.

"Mrs. Ortez," I said, a little hesitantly, "this is the president of the Coney Island Dragons. Jo-Jo, I'd like you to meet the lady who is putting me up for a while since I can't afford any place to sleep, just like you."

Then I asked Mrs. Ortez if Jo-Jo could stay with me a

few days in her home. She looked at her two little children, and she looked at the switchblade sticking out of Jo-Jo's pocket. Then she very kindly went over and put her arm around him and said, "Jo-Jo, you can sleep on the couch."

It was a brave thing, as anyone knows who has worked with these potentially violent boys. I took Jo-Jo aside and said, "Your clothes stink. We're in a home now, and we're going to have to do something. I've got eight dollars. We'll go to an Army-Navy store and get you a shirt and a pair of trousers."

I put on my other pair of shoes and took Jo-Jo to the nearest Army-Navy store we could find. He went into the back room of the store to change and simply left his old clothes where he stepped out of them. On the way back home, Jo-Jo looked at his reflection in every store window. "Not bad . . . not bad," he said.

So far, what I'd done with Jo-Jo was similar to what any social agency might have done. It was no doubt a good thing that this boy at last had a pair of shoes and a shirt, and that night he didn't have to sleep in the subway. But at heart, Jo-Jo was very much the same boy.

It took a change in me to bring about a change in Jo-Jo. And this change has affected both our lives ever since.

That evening at St. Nick's was as bad as ever. There was the usual breaking up, laughing, jeering. There were the usual fistfights and threats. There were the same sugges-tive gestures and lewd responses. Jo-Jo was there out of curiosity, watching it all.

Afterward, on the way back to the Ortez apartment, I was silent. I'd been hurt by the lack of response, and actu-ally, I was sulking.

"Preach, you're trying too hard."

It came just like that. From a homeless boy who pretended to be calloused through and through came a wonderful piece of insight.

The impact of those words went through me as if they had been spoken by God Himself.

Of course! *I* had been out there trying to change lives; I wasn't bringing the Holy Spirit to the gangs, I was bringing Dave Wilkerson. Even in giving Jo-Jo a pair of shoes *I* had been out in front. I knew in that moment that I would never be able to help Jo-Jo. I would never be able to help the gangs. All I could do was make an introduction, then step aside.

"You're trying too hard." The sudden insight brought a great burst of laughter that seemed to unsettle Jo-Jo.

"Cut it out, Preacher."

"I'm laughing, Jo-Jo, because you've helped me. From now on I'm not going to try so hard. I'm going to step aside and let the Spirit come through."

Jo-Jo was silent for a while. He cocked his head.

"I don't feel nothing," he said. "I don't expect to feel nothing, either."

We didn't speak again until we got upstairs to the Ortez apartment. Then suddenly again, with that direct way he had, Jo-Jo made me a deal.

"Look, Davie, you got a kid coming, right?"

I had told Jo-Jo that Gwen would be going to the hospital. The baby might be born any time.

"And you say there is a God and He loves me, right?"

"That's right," I said.

"All right, if there is a God, and if I pray to Him, He'll hear my prayers, right?"

"Absolutely."

"All right. What do you want, a boy or a girl?"

I could see the trap coming, but I didn't know what to do about it. "Now look, Jo-Jo, prayer isn't a slot machine where you put the right coin in and out comes the candy."

"In other words you're not so sure about this God business either."

"I didn't say that at all."

"What do you want? Boy or girl?"

I admitted that since we already had two girls we were hoping for a boy. Jo-Jo listened. Then Jo-Jo said a prayer: "Now, God, if You are up there and if You love me, give this preacher a boy."

That was Jo-Jo's prayer. It was a real one, and when he finished he was blinking hard. I was flabbergasted. I ran into my bedroom, and I began to pray as I hadn't prayed since I'd been in New York.

Jo-Jo and the Ortezes were sound asleep when the telephone call came at two thirty in the morning.

It was my mother-in-law. "David!" she said. "I couldn't wait until morning to call. I just had to tell you that you're a father! Do you want to know whether it was a boy or a girl?"

"More than you know."

"David, you've got a great big, strapping, ten-pound son."

Of course the skeptics will point out that there was statistically a fifty-fifty chance of Jo-Jo's prayer coming true. But something else was going on that night. When I went in and woke Jo-Jo with the news, he scratched his head.

"What do you know?" he said. "What do you know about that!"

Before the night was over, Jo-Jo was a changed boy. It

began with tears; Jo-Jo cried the bitterness out and he cried the hatred out. He cried out the doubts and the fears, too. When he was all through there was room for the kind of love the Christian knows, which doesn't depend on parents or preachers or even upon prayers being answered in the way we think they should be answered. From that day on, Jo-Jo had a love that was his for always, and he had taught me a lesson that was mine for always.

10

The auditorium was filling up on this final night of the rally. Far more young people had already come than had come on any previous evening. I saw some of the Chaplains; I saw the Dragons, and some GGIs. Among them, I was interested to note, was Maria. Nowhere could I see a Mau Mau, although I looked everywhere for their red jackets.

I hadn't been able to forget the appealing face and open manner of Israel, president of the Mau Maus. I'd personally invited this gang to the rally as my guests and hired a special bus for them. When I said I would reserve seats down front just for them, Israel promised to come and bring the others.

But it was the last night and they weren't here, and I thought I knew why. Nicky. He had stood seething and silent while Israel and I talked, exuding hatred of me and everything I stood for.

I wandered to a window overlooking the street. A bus was arriving. I knew it was the Mau Maus even before I saw them. I knew by the way the bus pulled into the curb, fast, as if the driver couldn't wait to get rid of his passengers. The doors opened. Out spilled nearly fifty teenagers, shouting and shoving. One boy tossed away an empty wine bottle as he stepped down.

Now the head usher came rushing up to me, excited and upset.

"Reverend, I don't know what to do." He drew me out onto the balcony and pointed down into the arena, where Israel and Nicky were making their way down the aisle, whistling and jeering as they came. "Those are Mau Maus," the head usher said. "I don't think I can keep them out of those reserved seats."

"That's all right," I said. "They're who the seats are for."

I left the usher staring after me and hurried downstairs to the dressing rooms. There I found an atmosphere of grave foreboding. "There are rival gangs out there," said the manager of the arena, "and we could have a full-scale rumble on our hands."

I looked out again. One of our own teenage girls, a remarkable young singer, as pretty as a movie star, was walking onto the center of the stage.

"Let's see how Mary does," I said. "Maybe we can soothe the savage beast with song."

But as Mary Arguinzoni began to sing, the hollering and whistling doubled. The boys and girls stood on their seats and began gyrating to the gospel song Mary sang. She looked over to where I was standing in the wings and asked with her eyes what she should do. Despite the cheers and the clapping and the calls for another song, I signaled to Mary that she should come away.

I walked out. It was a long walk to the center of the stage. Israel let me know he was there.

"Hey, Davie! I told you I'd come and bring my boys."

I turned to smile at him, and my eyes met the rock-hard gaze of Nicky. I had a sudden inspiration.

"We're going to do something different tonight," I announced over the loudspeaker system. "We're going to ask the gang members themselves to take up the collection." I looked right at Nicky as I spoke. "May I have six volunteers?"

Nicky was on his feet in a flash. He pointed at five Mau Maus and the six of them came forward and lined up in front of the stage. One result of my decision was apparent already: The arena had come to attention. Hundreds of teenagers stopped their cavorting and leaned forward in anticipation.

I stepped to the wings and took the paper milkshake cartons from the hands of the astonished ushers. "Now," I said to the boys as I handed them round, "when you've passed down the aisles, I'd like you to bring the offerings around behind that curtain and up onto the stage." I pointed to the place, watching Nicky's face. Behind that curtain there was a door to the street. A big arrow announced it: EXIT. Nicky accepted the carton solemnly, but in his eyes I could read mockery and contempt.

While the organ played, Nicky and his boys took up the collection. He did well as a fund-raiser. Nicky had sixteen stabbings to his record and was known as a vicious knife-fighter not only to the Brooklyn kids but to the gangs in Manhattan and the Bronx as well. When Nicky stood at the end of a row, shaking his carton, the kids dug deep.

When he was satisfied that he had enough, he signaled the other boys and together they walked down front and ducked behind the curtain. I waited, standing on the stage.

A wave of giggles swept over the room. A minute passed. Two minutes. Now the suppressed laughter exploded in guffaws, and the kids were on their feet, stamping and howling.

Then the room froze. I turned my head. Nicky and the others were crossing the stage toward me, the full cartons in their hands. Nicky looked at me with bewildered, almost frightened eyes, as though he himself could not understand what he was doing.

"Here's your money, Preacher," he said.

"Thank you, Nicky," I said, in what I hoped was a casual voice. I walked over to the pulpit as though I had not just lived through the worst two minutes of my life.

There was not a sound in the room as the six boys filed back to their places. I began to speak. I had gotten their ears, but I couldn't seem to get near their hearts.

I couldn't understand what was wrong. I'd spent hours preparing my sermon and prayed over every line of it. But I might as well have stood up and read the stock market report. Nothing I said seemed real to these kids; nothing came through to them. I preached for fifteen minutes, and all I could sense was the growing restlessness of the crowd. I reached the point in the sermon where I quoted Jesus' command to love one another.

Suddenly someone jumped up in the second row. He stood on his chair and shouted, "Hold on, Preacher! You say you want me to love them Dagos? One of them cut me with a razor. I'll love them all right—with a lead pipe."

Another boy, this one from the Hell Burners' section, jumped up and ripped open his shirt.

"I got a bullet hole here, Preacher. I know who did it. And you say we're supposed to love them? Man, you're not real."

It didn't sound real, not in that room so charged with hatred. It didn't sound humanly possible. "It isn't anything we can achieve through our own efforts," I admitted. "This is God's love I'm talking about. We have to ask Him to give us His kind of love. We cannot work it up by ourselves."

Suddenly, with brilliant clarity, I saw that these words were intended for me. Wasn't this the very lesson I'd learned from Jo-Jo? There's very little we humans can do to change ourselves or others, to heal them, to fill them with love instead of hate. We can bring our hearts and minds to God, but then we must leave them there.

I bowed my head. Right there I turned the meeting over. "All right, Jesus," I prayed, "there is nothing more that I can do. I invited these young people here; now I'm going to step out of the picture. Come, Holy Spirit. If You want to reach the hearts of any of these boys and girls, it will have to be through Your presence. Have Your own way, Lord."

I stood before that crowd with my head bowed for three minutes. I did not say a word. I did not move. I prayed. It didn't bother me anymore that some kids were laughing. Slowly the great hall began to quiet down. I recognized Israel's voice: "All right, you guys! Can it."

The quiet spread backward through the house and up to the balconies. That prizefight arena became totally silent.

Then I heard the sound of someone crying.

I opened my eyes. In the front row Israel pulled out a

handkerchief and blew his nose very loudly, then blinked and sniffed.

I continued praying, "Lord, sweep over this whole group."

Nicky got out his handkerchief. I couldn't believe my eyes and took another look. There he was, snorting and blinking and angry with himself for crying.

I knew the time had come to speak out. "All right. You've felt Him; He's here; He's in this room, come especially for you. If you want to have your life changed, stand up and come forward!"

Israel didn't hesitate. He stood up and faced his gang. "Boys," he said, "I've been your leader for three years. When I say go, you go! Right?"

"Right!" said the Mau Maus.

"I'm going forward and you're coming along. Get on your feet!"

They jumped up as one man and followed Israel forward. No, they raced him, elbowing each other to get there first. I looked to see if Nicky was among them. He was.

The surge forward was contagious. More than thirty boys from other gangs followed the Mau Maus downstairs to the dressing room where workers from the churches were ready. We were swamped. I kept going from room to room, helping where I could.

Suddenly I realized something peculiar. There were dozens of boys who had come forward for this new life, and only three girls. It was a puzzling thing. I suppose the girls, hearing us talk about love, didn't want to share love with anybody. They wanted to hold onto the shreds of "love" they did have.

The conversion hardest for me to believe was Nicky's.

There he stood, a great grin on his face, saying in his stammer, "I am giving my heart to God, Davie."

I couldn't believe him. The change was too sudden. He was puffing his perpetual cigarette, telling me that something new had happened in his heart.

I asked Israel and him to come with me, and I found copies of the Bible for them and each of the Mau Maus who had come forward. There were two sizes, little pocket editions and much larger ones. The boys didn't want the little ones.

"Give us them big books, Davie, so people can see what we're carrying."

With that, the boys lit up cigarettes, tucked their Bibles under their arms, and walked out.

Early the next morning Mrs. Ortez stuck her head in the door of my room. "Davie, it's the police on the phone."

My heart sank.

On the phone, the lieutenant asked me if I knew the Mau Mau gang. I said that I did. He asked if I'd come right down.

When I got to the Edward Street Precinct, there were half a dozen boys from the gang. I walked past them and introduced myself at the desk. What happened next I shall never forget.

The desk sergeant called the lieutenant, and the lieutenant assembled the whole force. The lieutenant stuck out his hand.

"Reverend," he said, "I want to shake your hand." I took his offer, and he pumped me firmly.

"How did you do it?" he asked. "These boys declared war on us a few months ago. They've given us nothing but trouble for years. Then this morning they all troop in here and you know what they want?"

I shook my head.

"They want us to autograph their Bibles!"

I looked at Nicky and Israel and the boys who were with them. They grinned at me.

"Anytime we can help you set up another street meeting, Reverend, just let us know," said the lieutenant. As we all stepped out onto the sidewalks of Brooklyn, I saw the sergeant sitting at his desk, shaking his head in wonder.

The boys, I learned, had been reading their Bibles most of the night. They were fascinated with the Old Testament stories particularly.

"Davie!" said Israel. "I'm in the Bible! Look, here's my name all over the place."

That night when I called Gwen at the hospital I was so full of the meetings I could hardly talk of anything else. "Last night made everything worthwhile, honey," I told her. "If only you could have been here!"

"Well, I've been kind of busy, Dave," she said. "Remind me to tell you about it sometime—when you get back to earth, that is."

11

I made the transition from the sweltering streets of New York to the coolness of the Pennsylvania hills in one swift turnpike jump. But every mile along the way I thought about Buckboard and Stagecoach, Nicky and Israel, Maria and Jo-Jo and Angelo: boys and girls whose lives had become so entwined in my own.

Back in Philipsburg, I sat in the shade of our backyard, watching my baby son in his basket under the trees. I caught my mind slipping back to kids in New York.

"Your parish is Philipsburg," Gwen reminded me gently one night, when I'd worried aloud for half an hour about Angelo Morales, who had made up his mind to be a preacher but had no money for school. "You mustn't neglect your own church."

Gwen was right, of course, and for the next six months I poured everything I had into my mountain parish. It was satisfying work and I loved it, but the other place was never very far from my thoughts.

"I've noticed," one of my parishioners told me, "you never

get quite as excited about things here as you do about those kids in the city."

I swallowed. I hadn't thought it showed.

But show it or not, I was getting trickles of an idea that alarmed me: that I take my family and move to New York as a full-time servant to these boys.

The idea was persistent with me. Was it possible that this urging to go to New York came from God? Was I truly supposed to abandon this parish and move Gwen and our three small children into the city with all its problems for daily living?

A definite and clear answer did not come right away. Like most guidance, it came to me one step at a time.

The first step was a return visit to New York.

"Do you realize that a year has passed since I was thrown out of the Farmer trial?" I asked Gwen one February morning.

"Uh-oh!" said Gwen.

"What do you mean by that?"

"You're getting ready to go back to New York, aren't you?"

I laughed. "Just overnight."

"Mm-hm."

It felt good to drive over the George Washington Bridge again, and later over the Brooklyn Bridge, and it felt good to walk through the streets again. I was surprised at how much at home I felt. I wanted to look up old friends. I wanted to revisit sites where miracles had happened in the hearts of boys.

One of these sites was the Fort Greene Projects. I was

walking down the street near there when suddenly I heard my name called.

"Davie! Preacher!"

I turned and saw two fine-looking young soldiers approaching me at a run. They were wearing neat, freshly pressed uniforms and their shoes shone till it hurt the eye.

I stared. "Buckboard! Stagecoach!" I hardly recognized them.

"Yes, sir," they said together, coming to a snappy attention. "Look good, eh, Davie?"

Buckboard, Stagecoach, and I had a great reunion. They told me they were doing well. They told me they quit the gang after our street meeting and never went back.

"In fact, Preach," said Stagecoach, "the Chaplain gang broke up for the rest of the summer. Nobody felt like fighting."

I left Buckboard and Stagecoach with real regret. I was surprised at the strength of my own reactions to this unexpected meeting. I had liked these boys and missed them more than I had known.

But the great surprise was ahead for me.

I set out down Edward Street, past the lamppost where Jimmy and I had preached, looking for Israel and Nicky. I saw a young lad I thought I recognized and asked him if he knew the whereabouts of Nicky and Israel of the Mau Maus.

The boy looked at me oddly. "You mean those jitterbuggers who turned saints?" He meant it as a joke, but my heart leaped.

"Nicky's crazy!" the boy continued with a disdainful snort. "He's going to be one of those nutty preachers."

I stood on the street with my mouth hanging open. "Nicky wants to become a *preacher*?"

"That's what he says."

I took off and looked for Nicky. I found him a little later, sitting on some apartment-house steps and talking to another boy.

"Nicky?" I said.

Nicky turned around, and I stared into a face I didn't know. Where the hard, defensive exterior had been, there was openness and animation. Now his eyes lit up with real joy.

"Preacher!" He hopped up and ran toward me. "Davie!" He turned to the boy who was with him. "Look, man! This is the preacher I told you about. This is the one who bugged me."

It was wonderful to see him. I asked Nicky if it was true that he wanted to go into the ministry.

Nicky looked down at the sidewalk. "I never wanted anything so bad, Davie," he said.

"This is terrific news!" I said. "Tell me, have you done anything about it yet?"

"I don't know how to start."

I was overflowing with ideas. I offered to write to some theological schools. I wanted to sponsor him myself. I wanted him to go to a voice clinic for his impeded speech. I even had some thoughts about raising the necessary money for all this. I had been invited to speak to a church group in Elmira, New York, a few weeks from then, on the problems of young people in the cities. It struck me as ironic that in that same city, Luis Alvarez had been imprisoned. He would be transferred by now; I had no idea where he was.

"Nicky," I said, "will you come with me to Elmira? Will you tell your story to the people there? It could be that they'll be able to help you."

I had no sooner made the suggestion than I began to have qualms about it. Nicky's story, as it had come to me in bits and pieces, was an exceedingly ugly one, full of brutality. I was accustomed by now to chilling sights and sounds on New York's streets, and even I found his story shocking.

Still, I argued with myself, the Elmira church had expressed a desire to learn about the gangs; here indeed would be a speedy introduction. For me it would mean a chance to hear Nicky's story from start to finish as I had not yet done.

A few weeks later, Nicky stood on a platform in Elmira, New York, to relate the story of his life. I had spent some time introducing him, stressing the poverty and loneliness that spawned boys like this so that the audience would not judge him before they heard him through.

My precautions were unnecessary. From the moment he began to speak, that roomful of people was with him. His own words, the sad narrowness of his experience, the flat recital by a boy who did not exaggerate or embellish, spoke volumes about the world he came from.

"I was mostly in the streets," he began, "because my parents had customers coming where we lived. They would come at night or in the day and then all of us kids had to go out. They were spiritualists, my parents. They advertised in the Spanish papers that they would talk with the dead and cure sickness, and they would also give advice about money and family problems.

"There was only one room at home, so us kids were in the street. At first the other kids beat me up, and I was afraid all the time. Then I learned how to fight, and they were scared of me and they left me alone. After a while I got so I liked it better in the street than I did at home. At home I was the youngest one. I was nothing. But in the street they knew who I was.

"My family moved a lot and mostly it was on account of me. If there was any trouble, the police would come around asking questions and then the superintendent wherever we lived would go to my parents and say we had to move. They didn't want their building to have trouble with the police. It was that way if the police just asked a Puerto Rican boy a question. It didn't matter if he did anything, the minute the police came around asking about him, he and his family had to get out.

"I didn't know why I acted like I did. There was a thing inside me that scared me. It worried me all the time, but I couldn't stop it. It was this feeling I got if I saw a cripple.

It was a feeling like I wanted to kill him. It was that way with blind people, too, or real little kids—anyone weak or hurt—I would hate them.

"One day I told my old man about this. He said I had a devil. He tried to call the devil out of me, but it wouldn't come.

"The crazy thing in me got worse and worse. If someone had crutches I would kick them, or if an old man had a beard I would try to pull it out, and I would rough up little kids. All the while I would be scared, but the thing inside me was laughing. The other thing was blood. The minute I saw blood I would begin to laugh and I couldn't stop it.

"When we moved into the Fort Greene Projects, I went in with the Mau Maus. They wanted me to be president. But in a rumble the president has to give orders and I wanted to fight. So they made me vice president.

"I was also sergeant-at-arms. That meant I was in charge of the arsenal. We had belts and bayonets and switchblades and zip guns. You steal a car aerial to make the zip guns. You use a door latch for the trip hammer and they shoot .22 shells.

"For rumbling I liked a baseball bat. I'd cut a hole in a garbage can to see out, then I'd put it over my head and swing the bat. The Mau Maus would never fight alongside me because when I got crazy like that I would beat on anybody.

"I also learned how to stick with a knife, which is when you cut someone but don't kill him. I stuck sixteen people, and I was in jail twelve times. Some of those times my picture was in the paper. When I walked down the street, everyone knew me, and the mothers would call their little kids.

"The gangs knew me, too. One day when I was waiting for a subway, five guys came up behind me. They got a leather belt around my neck and kept twisting it. I didn't die, but I used to wish I had because after that I could never talk right. There was a funny noise in my throat. I had this hate of people who had anything wrong with them, and now it was me.

"One day our gang was in a store on Flatbush Avenue. There were six of us, drinking soda, when seven Bishops walked in. The Bishop gang was at war with the Mau Maus.

"One of the Bishops went up to the counter like he owned it. I walked over and I shoved him. He shoved back and then everyone was fighting. The owner's wife started screaming. All the other customers ran out. There was a butcher knife on the counter. One of my boys picked it up and cut a Bishop five times through the scalp. I saw the blood and I started to laugh. I knew he was dead and I was scared, but I couldn't stop laughing. The owner's wife was telephoning the police. Another one of my boys picked up that butcher knife and hit her right in the stomach. Then we ran.

"I never touched the knife so I didn't go to jail. But my parents had to go to court, and I guess it was the first time they looked at me. They got scared when they saw what I was. They decided to go back to Puerto Rico. My brother and I went to the airport to say good-bye to them. On the way back from the airport in his car, he gave me a .32 pistol and said, 'You're on your own, Nick.'

"The first thing I had to do was find a place to sleep. I held up a guy with the gun and got ten dollars. I rented a room. I was sixteen then. That's how I lived after that, holding up guys for money or something to hock.

"During the day it was all right. I was with the gang. Whatever the president and I told them to do they would do. But at night, when I had to go into that room, it was terrible. I would think about the two dead people in the store. I would bang my head on the floor to stop thinking about them. I started waking up in the middle of the night crying.

"I turned eighteen in July 1958. That month the Dragons from the Red Hook Projects killed one of our boys. We were going down on the subway to get one of them. That's gang law: If one Mau Mau dies, one Dragon dies. We were walking the street on our way to the subway station when we saw a police car stopped and a whole bunch of Chaplains hanging around. The Chaplains are another gang in Fort Greene. We had a treaty with them that we wouldn't fight and we would work together if another gang invaded us.

"It looked like action so we went over. The Chaplains were all standing around two guys I never seen, one had a bugle and the other was a real skinny guy. Then somebody brought an American flag and the police car drove away. All it was, the two guys wanted to hold a street meeting.

"As soon as the flag came, the skinny guy got up on a chair, opened up a book, and this is what he read out of it: 'For God so loved the world, that he gave his only begotten Son, that whosoever believeth in him should not perish.'

"'Now,' the preacher said, 'I'm going to talk to you about "whosoever." "Whosoever" means African Americans and Puerto Ricans, and especially it means gang members.'

"I'd had enough. I said, 'Come on, you guys, we got business.'

"Not one of them moved. It was the first time they didn't follow me. Then I got scared, and I called that preacher every filthy name I knew. He paid no attention, just kept on talking, a long time.

"The next thing you knew the president of the Chaplains flopped down on his knees, right there, and started crying. The vice president and two warlords got down beside him and they cried. One thing I couldn't stand was crying. I was glad when the Chaplains left. I figured we would go, too.

"But then this preacher comes up to Israel—he was president of the Mau Maus—and starts shaking his hand. I figured he was trying to bust us up.

"So that preacher heads for me. 'Nicky,' he says, 'I love you.'

"No one in my life ever told me that. I didn't know what to do. 'You come near me, Preacher,' I said, 'I'll kill you!' And I meant it. Israel and the preacher talked some more, but at last he left and I thought it was over.

"But later this preacher came back and he talked about this big meeting for gangs they were going to have up in Manhattan, and how we should come. 'I'll send a bus for you,' says the preacher. So then Israel said we'll come.

"I said, not me. I'd rather die than go to that meeting. But when the gang went, it turned out I was with them. I was scared not to be with the gang. When we got there here were three rows of seats right down front roped off for us. The preacher said he'd save us seats but I never figured he'd do it.

"A lady was playing the organ and I got the guys stamping and shouting. Then a girl came out on the stage and began to sing. I whistled at her and everyone laughed. It was all going my way and I was feeling good.

"Finally the preacher came out and he said, 'Before the message tonight we're going to take up a collection.'

"I figured I saw his angle. I'd been wondering all along what was in this for him. Now I saw he was a money-grabber like everyone else.

"'We're going to ask the gang members themselves to take it up,' he says. 'They'll bring the money around behind this curtain and up onto the stage.'

"Anyone could see there was a door back there!

"'May I have six volunteers?' he says.

"Man, I was on my feet in a second. I pointed out five of my boys and we piled down there quick. Here was my chance to make him look silly. He gave us cardboard cartons.

"We worked that whole arena. If I didn't like what someone put in, I stood there till he gave some more. They all knew Nicky. Then we met down behind the curtain.

"There was the door. It was wide open. Back in the arena some of them were laughing. They knew what we were pulling. My boys were watching me, waiting for the word to cut out.

"But I stood there. I didn't know what it was; I had a funny feeling. Suddenly I knew what it was: That preacher trusted me. That never happened in my life before.

"Inside, I could hear they were giving him a hard time. They were shouting and stamping, and he was having to stand there and face them, trusting me.

"'All right, you guys,' I said. 'We're going up on that stage.'

"They looked at me like I wasn't right in my head, but they never argued. We went up the stairs and you never heard a place get quiet so fast. We gave him the cartons. 'Here's your money, Preacher,' I said.

"He just took the money, like he knew all the time I'd bring it.

"I went back to my seat and I was thinking harder than I ever thought before. He started talking and it was all about the Holy Spirit. The preacher said the Holy Spirit could get inside people and make them clean. He said it didn't matter what they'd done, the Holy Spirit could make them start new, like babies.

"Suddenly I wanted that so bad I couldn't stand it. It was as if I was seeing myself for the first time. All the filth and the hate like pictures in front of my eyes.

"'You can be different!' he said. 'Your life can be changed!'

"I wanted that, I needed that, but I knew it couldn't happen to me. The preacher told us to come forward if we wanted to be changed but I knew it was no use.

"Then Israel told us all to get up. 'I'm president,' he said, 'and this whole gang is going up there!'

"I was the first one at the rail. I kneeled down and said the first prayer of my life and this was it: 'Dear God, I'm the dirtiest sinner in New York. I don't think You want me. If You do want me, You can have me. As bad as I was before, I want to be that good for Jesus.'

"Later the preacher gave me a Bible and then I went home wondering if the Holy Ghost was really inside me, and how I would know. The first thing that happened, when I went in my room and shut the door, I didn't feel scared.

"The next day everyone was staring because word had gone around that Nicky had religion. But another thing happened that made me know it was real. Little kids would always run when they saw me, but on that day two little boys stared at me a minute and then they came right up to me. They wanted me to measure and see which one of them was taller—nothing important. But then I knew I was different, even if it didn't show except to kids.

"Then, a few weeks later, a Dragon came up to me and he said, 'Is it true you don't carry weapons anymore?' I told him it was true, and he pulled a ten-inch knife and went for my chest. I threw my hand up and caught the knife there. I don't know why, but he ran, and I stood there, looking at the blood coming from my hand. I remembered how blood always made me go crazy, but that day it didn't. Words came into my mind that I had read in my Bible, 'The blood of Jesus Christ cleanseth us from all sin.' I ripped my shirt and tied up my hand and from that day blood never bothered me."

As Nicky talked, a hush fell over the room—because Nicky's voice, the straining, stammering voice in which he had begun his story, had altered as he spoke. Gradually the words came more readily, the sounds clearer, until he was speaking as distinctly and effortlessly as anyone in the room. Only now did Nicky himself realize it. He stood on the platform trembling, tears streaming down his face.

I never knew what had caused his speech problem. Nicky, of course, had never considered seeing a doctor about it. I only know that, from that night on, his voice was healed.

That night, too, a collection was taken in Elmira that started Nicky on a remarkable journey.

12

I sat in my study at Philipsburg looking back on the last few months. I had written to the Latin American Bible Institute in La Puente, California, about Nicky's dream of the ministry. I made no bones about his past, and I acknowledged frankly that he had not been in his new life long enough to prove himself. Would they, I asked them, accept him as a student on probation?

They wrote back that they would. Not only that, but they found themselves so intrigued with this story of transformation in a boy from the streets that not long afterward they invited Angelo Morales to come to school there, too. Buckboard and Stagecoach were doing well, and now Nicky and Angelo were on their way to becoming ministers.

But in the spring of 1959 came news that pulled me to my feet again and put me back on the path I had imagined would be a short one.

Israel was in jail.

For murder.

I drove to New York to see Israel's mother.

"My boy, he was so good for a while," said Israel's mother, rocking from side to side in distress. "He settle down and when school start he do his studies. But then the gang start up again. Do you know what it is, the 'draft'?"

I knew. When gangs were starting, or when their ranks were depleted for one reason or another, any boy in the neighborhood was simply drafted. He was stopped on the street and told that as of that moment he was a gang member. If he refused?

First, a simple beating. If he still refused, his thumbs or an arm was broken. If he refused again, his life was threatened. Most boys join up. Israel was actually fired at a number of times before he went back to the gang.

"My boy, he so scared," said Israel's mother. "One night there was a big fight. One of the other boys got killed. Israel did not shoot him, but he was with those killers, so they put him in jail."

Israel's mother showed me a letter from him, much handled and spotted with tears. He said he was sorry for her sake. He didn't seem bitter. He talked about the day when he would be getting out. He even spoke about me, saying that he would be "sad for the preacher, when he finds out. Tell Davie I'd like to hear from him."

How could we have kept Israel out of jail? Would it have helped to have me nearer, to give advice and friendship? Would it have helped to take him away from this neighborhood, away from the gang that drafted him and the life that poisoned him?

I asked Israel's mother this, and she shook her head. "I don't know," she said. "My boy wanted to be good, Mr. Wilkerson."

Night and day he was on my mind. I talked to Gwen about him. I found myself asking people at the church what they would have done for him where I failed. I wrote him, but found that he could not write back. He could write only to his immediate family. Every day I went up to my mountain to pray for Israel. I could do nothing else for him.

In the meantime, I told his story to others, asking them what might have been done differently. Time and again the same answer came back: follow up.

But to follow up meant to be on the scene.

A turning point in my life was at hand. And then it happened.

It was a hot August night, a year and a half after my first trip to New York. I was standing in the pulpit at the Wednesday evening prayer service, when suddenly my hands began to tremble. The thermometer read 85 degrees, but I was shaking as if I had a chill. Instead of feeling troubled or sick, however, I felt exhilaration. It was as if the Spirit of the Lord was drawing near, in that room.

I still don't know how I managed to get through the service. But before I knew it the congregation was filing out to go home. At ten thirty I closed up the church and left by the rear door. What happened next was one of those vivid moments that I shall never forget as long as I live.

The moon was shining with an unusual brilliance. It bathed the sleeping town in its cold and mysterious light; but there was one spot in particular that seemed illuminated. In back of the church there was a four-acre field that had been planted in grain. The wheat now stood about a foot and a half high. I found myself propelled into the very center of this field of grain, swaying in the night breeze.

I found myself quoting the biblical figure of the harvest: "Look, I tell you, look round on the fields; they are already white, ripe for harvest" (John 4:35 NEB).

In my mind's eye I saw each of the blades of wheat as a youngster on the streets of the city, hungry for a new beginning. Then I turned and looked at the church and the parsonage where Gwen and the three children were, safe, happy, secure. But a quiet inner voice spoke to me as clearly as if a friend had been standing nearby. *The church is no longer yours*, I was told. *You are to leave.*

I looked at the parsonage, and the same inner voice said, *This home is no longer yours. You are to leave.*

I answered, "Yes, Lord. I shall go."

I walked over to the parsonage, and there was Gwen, waiting up. I could tell something had happened to her, too.

"What is it, Gwen?"

"David," Gwen said, "you don't have to tell me. I know already. You're going to leave the church, aren't you?"

I looked at Gwen and said nothing.

"I heard it, too, David," she continued. "We're going, aren't we?"

In the darkness I put my arms around her. "Yes, my dear. We're going."

The following Sunday I stood in the pulpit and looked out at the faces of the people we knew so well.

"My friends," I said, "as you know, these have been five extraordinarily happy and wonderful years for me, for my wife and for our children.

"But an unusual thing happened last Wednesday night— something that can have but one explanation."

I told the congregation of my experience in the grain field, and of Gwen's amazing parallel experience inside the parsonage. I told them that I did not doubt this to be the voice of the Lord, and that we would have to obey. I couldn't answer their questions about where we would go. I suspected it would be New York, but I wasn't sure. All I knew was that we were to leave Philipsburg now, without delay.

That very afternoon when I returned to the parsonage, the telephone began to ring. One call was from Florida, from a pastor who said that he couldn't shake the urging to invite me to come and conduct a series of retreat meetings for him immediately. Another call came, then another, and before the day was over I found myself booked for twelve weeks of speaking engagements around the country. Within three weeks we had stored our furniture and moved from the parsonage into four rooms in my wife's parents' house.

For the next several months, I held meetings all across the nation. Whenever possible I chose engagements that would take me near New York City, that huge, congested, anguish-filled city I so loved.

In 1960, one of these engagements took me to Irvington, New Jersey, where I met Pastor Reginald Yake. I told him, as I told everyone, about some of the experiences I had had in New York. He listened intently and asked questions for an hour.

"Dave," he said at last, "it seems to me that the churches need a full-time worker among the gangs in New York. I'd like to make a few telephone calls to some friends in the city."

One of the men he called was Stanley Berg, co-pastor of Glad Tidings Tabernacle near Penn Station. A meeting of interested clergymen was scheduled in the basement of Mr. Berg's church, and I was invited to come.

At the meeting, someone read a letter from the police commissioner urging the churches to take a stronger stand in matters affecting young people. Mr. Berg stood and spoke about the work I had already been doing. Then I got up and talked about the direction in which I thought work among teenagers might now go.

That day, a new ministry was born, with a main purpose of reaching young boys and girls with the message of God's love. We called the new ministry Teen-Age Evangelism. I had already been involved in this work, so I was voted director of the organization. A police captain named Paul DiLena was voted secretary-treasurer. Poor Paul: He wasn't at the meeting to defend himself.

Next came the question of money. We figured that for office space, printing, salaries and so forth, we gave ourselves a budget of $20,000. Of course, there was no actual *cash* represented, as our secretary-treasurer discovered a few moments later when Stanley Berg called him to inform him of his victory at the polls.

"Paul," said Pastor Berg, "there's good news. You have just been elected treasurer of Teen-Age Evangelism. David Wilkerson is your director in this fight for young people. And you'll be glad to hear that you've got a budget of $20,000 for the first year."

Captain DiLena said, "Who is David Wilkerson, who's got the books, and where is the money?"

"Paul," said Pastor Berg, "we have no books, we have no money, and Dave Wilkerson is a preacher from the hills of Pennsylvania who believes he belongs in New York."

Paul laughed. "You make it sound naïve," he said.

"We are naïve, Paul," said Pastor Berg. "About as naïve as David was when he stepped up to Goliath with nothing but a sling, a pebble, and the conviction that he was on God's side."

13

It was a blustering February morning two years from that other February when I sold the television set and found myself launched on this strange adventure.

I was standing on the Staten Island Ferry, hardly realizing myself what a giant stride we had just made toward my dream. Spume splashed up on the deck from a choppy sea. Off to starboard was the Statue of Liberty, and I found myself thinking how appropriate it was that I would pass her each morning. Because I was going to Staten Island on a specific and hopeful mission: to rent offices for our new program aimed at setting youngsters free.

I had an address in my pocket that sounded appropriate as the site for our headquarters suite: 1865 Victory Boulevard. But when I got to this "headquarters suite," I had to smile. It consisted of a grubby outer office, an inner office, and a shipping room in a less-than-chic neighborhood.

Teen-Age Evangelism started in these three rooms. We had one paid employee: myself. And I didn't receive enough salary to afford even a room in the cheapest boardinghouse.

I set up a couch next to my desk. I ate what I could cook on a hot plate or, on occasions, with friends around New York who would look at my slender frame and ask me to share a meal with them.

But the part of the arrangement that was hardest was having the family divided. Gwen remained in Pittsburgh with her folks, and she longed to join me at the earliest moment.

"I know what you're doing is right, Dave," she said on one of our visits-by-telephone. "But I'm lonesome. Gary's growing up without even knowing what you look like." We agreed that we would move the family to New York as soon as the school year was over.

In the meantime, I found my new home was a perfect place for prayer. There was nothing to offer distraction. Furniture consisted of a desk, a hard straight-backed chair and my couch. I found it was a pleasure to pray in this setting of austerity, and each night I looked forward to my old television-viewing time—midnight to two in the morning—as a time of renewal. Never did I get up without being refreshed, encouraged and filled with new enthusiasm.

Those early days were exciting. The Spanish- and English-speaking Assemblies churches in the New York area had supplied me with $1,000 to launch our work. I used most of this money conducting two experiments. The first we called "Operation Saturation." This was a literature program aimed at reaching every high school student in the city's trouble areas and tackling the problems they faced on the street by offering help from the Bible. We worked hard on this program, bringing hundreds of young people from local churches into the operation to distribute our booklets. At the end of three months, however, we could point to only a handful of teenagers who had been truly changed as a result.

So we turned to our second experiment: television. I gathered together one hundred boys and girls who had been in trouble and had found the way out. We formed an all-teenage choir and every week for thirteen weeks we put on a television show. The format was simple. The kids sang, then one of them told his or her story.

We were encouraged by the ratings this show received: We were apparently very popular among the teenagers of the city. But television was expensive. Kids all over the metropolitan area sent in their nickels and dimes to help support the show, but even so, at the end of our first thirteen weeks we were $4,500 in debt.

"It looks like we're going to have to cancel the series before we can really measure results," I said to our committee, in a special meeting called to consider the crisis. We wanted to continue the experiment for another thirteen weeks, but there didn't seem to be a way.

Suddenly a man I had never seen before stood up in the rear of the meeting.

"I would like to make a suggestion," this gentleman said. He introduced himself to us: He was the Reverend Harald Bredesen, a Dutch Reformed minister from Mount Vernon, New York. "I've seen your shows, and they have a fresh quality about them that I like. Before you decide definitely to cancel, I wonder if you'd come talk to a friend of mine."

I agreed.

The next day Harald and I went to visit Chase Walker, a magazine editor in Manhattan. Mr. Walker listened attentively to the story of our work and how it got started. He seemed interested, but at the end of the conversation, he also seemed puzzled.

"Just what is it you want me to do?" he said.

"I'll be honest with you," said Harald. "We want $10,000."

Mr. Walker blanched. So did I.

Then Mr. Walker began to laugh. "Well, I appreciate the compliment, but I certainly don't have $10,000. How did you happen to think of me in connection with this need?"

"I can't really answer that question," said Harald. "I've had the most remarkable feeling, ever since I learned that this program might have to be canceled, that somehow you held the key. Every time I'd think about it I'd think, Chase Walker! Nothing more specific than that." Harald paused hopefully. Mr. Walker said nothing. "Well," said Harald, "I was wrong. But these hunches, when they come so strong, usually mean something."

Mr. Walker rose from his chair, bringing the interview to a close. "I'll let you know if I get any ideas. In the meantime, thanks for sharing the story with me."

We were out the door of his office, when suddenly Mr. Walker called us back. "Wait a moment."

We turned around and went back into Walker's office. "Something just occurred to me. I got a telegram today I don't understand at all." He fished around among the papers on his desk and came up with it. It was from W. Clement Stone, president of the Combined Insurance Company of Chicago, a friend of Walker's. "Disregard previous telegram," it said. "I will be at the Savoy Hilton Wednesday."

"That's today," said Mr. Walker. "But I never got any previous telegram. We had no plans to get together. I wondered whether his secretary got my name confused with someone else's."

Walker looked at Harald for a moment, then picked up a pen and scribbled a note. "Go up to the Savoy," he said, handing us the note in an unsealed envelope. "Ask for Mr. Clement Stone. If he's in, you can use this as an introduction, and see what develops. Read it if you want to."

We did, waiting for the elevator out in the hall. "Dear Clem," it said. "This is to introduce David Wilkerson, who is doing a remarkable job with teenagers in this city. David needs $10,000 for his work. You might listen to his story carefully, and, if it interests you, help him out. Chase."

Twenty minutes later we were knocking on the door of a suite in the Savoy. A gentleman came to the door tying a large bow tie. He was obviously dressing for dinner.

"Mr. Stone?"

The man nodded.

"Excuse us, we have a note for you from Chase Walker."

Mr. Stone stood in the doorway and read the note, then asked us in. He seemed as puzzled as we were about the situation. He said he was due downstairs in a few moments, but that if we wanted to talk while he finished dressing, he'd be glad to listen.

Fifteen minutes later, Mr. Stone was ready to leave, and I had barely launched into a description of Teen-Age Evangelism.

"I have to go now," said Mr. Stone gently. "But if Chase Walker recommends you, that's good enough for me. I like the sound of your work. Send me your bills. I'll pay them up to ten thousand."

Harald and I looked at each other, stunned.

"Now if you'll excuse me, please." Mr. Stone edged toward the door. "I'll pay you a visit next time I'm in New York, and we'll work out details . . ." and he was gone.

The $10,000 went toward our debt, and it also paid for the second thirteen weeks, and for a film, *Vulture on My Veins*, about drug addiction among teenagers in New York. But this money purchased more than just film and television time. It bought us new respect for this ministry. It was becoming increasingly clear to us that the hand of the Lord was in our work.

14

In spite of the success of our television show, after about
six months I began to feel strongly that we were miss-
ing one vital ingredient: personal contact.

I started going out on the streets and talking to teenagers
face-to-face. As soon as I did, I knew that I had touched
the key to effective work with people. Jesus did not have
television or the printed word to help Him. His was a face-
to-face ministry. I knew as soon as I returned to going out
into the streets that this was the method meant for me, too.

Each morning I closed the door at my headquarters on
Victory Boulevard, stepped onto the ferry and then onto
the subway, and as soon as I arrived in Brooklyn, I simply
started talking with the boys I met. Time and again, they
responded. I could once again watch the change taking
place before my eyes.

More and more I realized we had to act on the problem
of follow-up. With most of the youngsters I was satisfied
if I got them established in a good local church. But with

boys who were in serious trouble, or who had no home, some closer form of follow-up was needed.

One morning after I'd stepped off the ferryboat in Manhattan, I walked downstairs to the subway that would take me over to Brooklyn. The subway at this point makes a great loop, and in the turn its wheels scream. This place will always have a special meaning for me. Because there, among the screams of the subway, I suddenly saw my old dream take on substance.

It sprang, full-grown, to mind. The house I had dreamed of—we might call it the Teen Challenge Center—would be located in the heart of the roughest part of the city. It would be headquarters for a dozen or more full-time workers who shared my hopes for the young people around us, who saw their wonderful potential and their tragic waste. Each worker would be a specialist: one would work with boys from the gangs, another with boys who were addicted to drugs, another would work with parents. There would be women workers who would specialize in girl gang members, girls with addictions, and other problems.

We could bring in boys and girls who needed special help. They would live in an atmosphere of discipline and affection. They would participate in our worship. They would watch Christians living together, working together; and they would be put to work themselves. It would be a center where they were prepared for the life of the Spirit.

In the summer of 1960, after I'd been working full-time in the city for close to a year, I began to talk about my dream aloud. On fund-raising trips, I preached about the need. Among our churches in New York I painted the picture as I had envisioned it. But always I was met with the same comment. "Dave, this dream has one flaw: It requires money."

This was true. We never seemed to have more than a hundred dollars in our account at any one time. It took a good hard scolding from Gwen to shake me free from the fear of launching forth just because we had no money.

Gwen came to New York as soon as the school year was over in Pittsburgh. I found an apartment near the office in Staten Island. "It's not exactly the Hilton," I said to Gwen on the phone, "but at least we'll be together. Get packed— I'm coming to get you."

"Darling," said Gwen, "I don't care if we live in the street, just as long as we live there together."

So Gwen came east. We crowded all our furniture into four rooms again, but we were extremely happy. Gwen followed all the moves of the new ministry. She was particularly interested in my dream of a working family with a center of its own.

"David," she said one night, after I had complained again about lack of funds, "you're going at this backward. You're trying to raise your money first, and then buy your home. If you're doing this in faith, you should commit yourself to your center first, then raise your money for it."

The more I thought about it, the more it reminded me of biblical stories. Wasn't it always true that man had to act first, often with what seemed a foolish gesture, before God performed His miracles? Moses had to stretch his arm over the sea before it parted; Joshua had to blow some horns before the walls of Jericho fell; perhaps I had to commit myself to the purchase of a new center before the miracle could come to pass.

I got together with my central committee, which consisted of six ministers and three laymen. All had wonderful spiritual vision and were willing to give time to our organization.

I told them of the growing need for a home where gang members and narcotics addicts could associate with Christian workers. I told them about Gwen's feeling that we ought to commit ourselves to a place first, then worry about paying for it later. The committee was willing to go along with the idea. "We can think of it as an open experiment in faith," suggested Arthur Graves, one of the ministers.

This is what happened immediately following our decision:

On December 15, 1960, at two o'clock in the morning while I was deep in prayer, I received the sudden clear impression that there was a particular street in Brooklyn we were supposed to investigate. We knew that our home should be close to the heart of the troubled Bedford-Stuyvesant area, so we had been making our first inquiries along Fulton Street. But now came the name Clinton Avenue. I got out a map and located the street.

The next day I called several of the members of the committee, and we agreed to meet on Clinton Avenue to see what kind of houses, if any, might be available. Before I set out, I called Paul, our treasurer, and asked how much money the organization had available.

"Why?" asked Paul.

"We thought we'd go look at houses on Clinton Avenue."

"Jolly," said Paul. "Right now we have a balance of $125.73."

The first house we looked at seemed to fit our needs, and the price of $17,000 seemed reasonable. An old gentleman showed us around. We actually got to the stage of talking money with him. The terms sounded good. But when we came back the next day, the old gentleman began to stall. This went on for several days until finally we felt we were supposed to look elsewhere.

We looked at another house on Clinton Avenue that had a "For Sale" sign in a window. We had less than a hundred dollars in the bank now. And this time, instead of looking at a $17,000 house, we were talking to the owner of a $34,000 property. It had been a nursing home and in many ways was ideal for the center—completely furnished with beds, offices, and accommodations for staff. The man came down in his price, too, while we were talking to him. I was ready to sign up.

"Before we make any decisions," said Dick Simmons, a young minister on our board, "I have the key to a house across the street. I think we ought to look at it."

"How much is it?" I asked.

Dick hesitated. "It's $65,000."

"Great," I said. "Every time we look at a house, the price goes up."

The $65,000 house was a mansion. I must admit my heart leaped when I saw it. It was a stately Georgian house built of red brick and as solid-looking as Monticello.

What a shock awaited us, though, when we stepped inside.

The house had been unoccupied for two years. For several

years before that, students from a nearby college had used it for wild parties.

Now a squatter lived in the place, illegally. He was a hoarder, and he had filled every room in the house with junk: newspapers, bottles, skeleton umbrellas, baby carriages, and rags. Each morning he set out with a grocery cart, collecting trash, which he would tote back into the house and stash.

Most of the water pipes were broken, plaster fell from the ceilings and walls, banisters lolled on their sides, and doors were ripped from their hinges. But you could still see that this had once been a truly regal home. There was a private elevator to the second floor. There was a whole attic of servants' quarters. The basement was dry and sound, as were the walls.

We walked through the debris, silent, until all of a sudden, in a loud and clear voice, Harald Bredesen said, "This is the place God wants for us." There was something so commanding about his voice that it had the quality of prophecy.

Dick Simmons returned the keys to the owners, and he told them frankly that a price of $65,000 might be appropriate for the house in perfect condition, but had they seen it lately? The owners came down in their price. Dick talked some more. The owners came down again. Eventually Dick had brought the asking price down to $42,000!

We had one hundred dollars in the bank. But if we were intended to move into this house, who was I to object?

That night, during my prayer time, I placed the question before the Lord.

"You have helped me know Your will in the past, Lord, by giving me a sign." I thought back to when I wondered whether to sell the television set. "I'd like to put another fleece before You, Lord."

The next day I went down to Glad Tidings and had a long talk with Mrs. Marie Brown, co-pastor with Stanley Berg of the fine old church. I told her again about our reason for wanting a center, and I described to her the building we had found.

"David," said Mrs. Brown, "this has every feel of being right. If you were to buy the building, when would you need the binder?" The binder was an offer in writing.

"Within one week."

"Would you like to come to church Sunday afternoon and make an appeal?"

It was a tremendous opportunity, and I was glad to say I would come. But still, I wanted to know for sure that God was in our plans. I knew that the most Glad Tidings had ever raised for home missions at a single request was $2,000. We needed more than twice that amount. The 10 percent down payment alone would come to $4,200.

"Lord," I said that night in prayer, "if *You* want us to have that building, You can let us know for sure by allowing us to raise that in a single afternoon." I went on, like Gideon, to make things more difficult. "And furthermore, Lord, let me raise that amount without mentioning how much we need." I paused. "And furthermore," I said, "let me raise it without even making an appeal. Let this be something the people do out of their own hearts."

After I'd put all those fleeces before the Lord, I waited to see what would happen.

Sunday afternoon arrived. I preached a very simple sermon. Deliberately, I tried to make it as factual as I could, stating our problem and our hope. I told the stories of a few boys we had reached. At the end of the service, I said: "Folks, I'm not going to make an emotional appeal. I want this to be of the Spirit if it's to be done at all. He knows what we need. I'm going to leave now and go down into the basement. If it should occur to you that you want to give a certain amount to this work, I'll be glad to hear from you."

I went downstairs to the basement and waited. Minutes slipped away, and there was no sound of steps on the stairs. Two more minutes passed. Five. Ten whole minutes went by and I gave up.

Then the door at the end of the hall opened softly. In stepped an old lady with tears in her eyes. "Reverend Wilkerson," she said, "I've been praying for fifteen years for this work to be raised up. Here's ten dollars. It's all I can give, but I know it will multiply and be greatly used."

Before she left, the back door opened again, and a steady stream came in. The next person was a lady who said, "Reverend Wilkerson, I've been paid some money from Social Security. I want to give it to your boys."

The next person to come up was a man; he gave us two hundred dollars. The next gave three hundred dollars. A little boy came up and said he had only fourteen cents, but he said, "God is in this. You're getting all I got."

A schoolteacher came up and said, "David, I don't make much money, but I do work with teenagers like you do. I know what you're up against. I'd like to donate 25 dollars."

It took fifteen minutes for the line to walk through and lay its money on the desk. But each person brought more than just money; he or she brought encouragement, and above all they all brought a real joy to their giving, so that I felt the joy, too. When, finally, the last person left, I took the pile of bills and checks up to Mrs. Brown's office where we counted it. The amount? Four thousand four hundred dollars!

I told Mrs. Brown then about the fleeces I had put before the Lord. She was as excited as I. She was more convinced than ever that God was in the project.

The one thing that I did not confide to Mrs. Brown was my puzzlement over that extra two hundred dollars. We'd asked for $4,200 for the binder and we'd received $4,400. Why were we given that extra two hundred dollars?

A few days later, I was talking over the final costs of putting down our binder with our attorney, Julius Fried. I handed him the check for $4,200.

Julius moved uneasily in his chair. "You know of course that I'm not charging the center anything for my services. . . . But the other lawyers have to be paid, and we're going to need some unexpected money. We'll have to have the check at the time we put down the binder."

"How much, Julius?"

"Two hundred dollars."

The rest of the money for the balance of the $12,000 down payment we had agreed upon came to us in an equally peculiar manner. The following Sunday, at Bethpage, Long Island, a congregation came streaming forward at the close of the meeting and pressed over $3,000 into my hands. The following week, Arthur Graves called me to announce a decision his church had made. "David," he said, "my board has voted to send me to the closing with a blank check. You can fill it in for the amount needed to close the deal."

That is how it worked out that God provided us with precisely the amount we needed for the creation of the Teen Challenge Center. Down to the penny, we were provided for. On the day we were handed the keys to the beautiful mansion on Clinton Avenue, I said to my wife, "Gwen, you were right. Do you realize that within just one month from the time you challenged me to step out in faith, we have raised $12,200?"

Gwen was as pleased as I. "When is the second mortgage due?" she asked.

"Not until fall."

It was months away. But that due date on the $15,000 second mortgage would be upon us in no time.

15

It was unbelievable how much junk one man could accumulate. We discovered whole rooms we did not even know existed because the door was covered with ceiling-high piles of debris.

Gwen came down to look over the property with me. "Why don't you get some of the pastors to set up a youth work party?"

That's what we did. One Saturday morning toward the end of January, three cars pulled up and out swarmed fifteen young boys and girls jabbering and yelling and proclaiming that they'd make short shrift of any junk we showed them. When they went in and were taken from attic to basement, I watched the enthusiasm drain out of them.

But those kids did a wonderful job. They started at the front of the building and cleared a path for themselves, and room by room, floor by floor, they kept steadily at it until they had carried every bit of that junk out into the backyard.

Paul DiLena alerted the sanitation department of the job

ahead of them. "I think there will be at least four truckloads of trash to haul off," he said.

The trucks arrived at 416 Clinton on schedule, but the men did not start working. The junk piled high on the sidewalk and street, and the sanitation crew just stood around. When Paul saw what was happening, he caught on. They expected a tip.

"All right," he said, "how much do you want?"

"Thirty dollars."

Paul shrugged as one used to the ways of New York. Rather than hold the project up, he would pay the tip himself—when the job was done.

Hours later the last of the trucks was filled. Six garbage trucks had rumbled down the street, groaning under their burden. The foreman came and asked Paul if everything was all right.

"Perfect," said Paul. "You did a good job." He reached for his wallet.

The foreman gave a forced laugh. "Look, mister, these kids told me what you're doing here. I've got a teenager of my own. Do you think we'd take *money* for helping you out?"

With that he got into his truck, revved it up, and stormed away with a show of one who was really pretty tough.

At the end of three weeks, we were finally ready to begin work on the house itself. Painters from various churches arrived, and room by room we covered up the graffiti on the walls. Then plumbers came. They had to tear the walls apart as new frozen and burst pipes were discovered. All this cost money, which I raised by taking time out for flights

all over the country to make appeals. One blow came when the city announced that before we could get a certificate of occupancy, a complete sprinkler system had to be installed in the building. The cost: five thousand dollars.

Off I flew again, taking time out from the work I really wanted to do, to raise money. But I could never have done all the fund-raising by myself. Everyone on the board helped in his own way.

Finally, the last painter and the last plumber left the center. God had raised up this home. Now we had to put it to use. We wanted to fill it with His children. Before we could do that, we had to give His children a place to sit down. We had a fine building, but there was nothing in it.

At this stage of our experience I realized how much God wanted all sorts of people to be a part of our work. We started mostly as an Assemblies of God program, and before we knew it, we had an Episcopalian and a Presbyterian and a Baptist and a Dutch Reformed committee member.

We had also attracted the interest of some influential businessmen.

One business friend of the Teen Challenge Center was Grant Simmons Jr., president of the Simmons Bed Company. We were introduced to Mr. Simmons and went to him with a specific request. We needed twenty beds. For an hour we sat in Mr. Simmons' Park Avenue offices telling him about our hopes and about the strange way God was working in the city. Mr. Simmons was generous. From that day on, many a boy who was used to sleeping on subway benches slept at the center on Simmons beds and mattresses.

We planned to use the home in this way: Eventually we would have twenty workers at the center. Each morning these young men and women would rise, have breakfast, and then spend the morning in prayer and study. This would be essential. I had long ago discovered that too much running around, without a base of quiet meditation, produces little.

After lunch, our street day would begin. Teams of two or three workers would start walking over a prescribed route, keeping an eye out for signs of trouble. They would be trained to spot the symptoms of narcotics addiction; they would be on the lookout for the teenage alcoholic, or for the girl runaway. They would talk to gang members, especially the members of fighting gangs.

They would go not with an eye to gaining converts but with an eye to meeting need. The conversions would take care of themselves. If we really met a human need, the world would beat a path to our door.

Most of the teenagers we contacted in this way would never live at the center. We would put them in touch with a minister near their home and work through him. We would follow up regularly until it was clear these youngsters could stand on their own.

But some boys and girls would need special attention. They would be brought to the center, the boys to live in the top-floor dormitory with the male workers on our staff; the girls to live on the second floor with the women and the married members of our staff. We expected to be working mostly with boys, but if a girl was in need we would not turn her away.

The key to this whole plan lay with the workers. Where

was I going to find twenty bright and aggressive yet em-pathetic and healthy young men and women, who would work for very little? Who would literally risk their lives?

As if in answer to this question, I received an invitation from Central Bible College in Springfield, Missouri, to go there for a lecture. I flew out and presented the challenge of our streets to the student body. It was a wonderful ser-vice in which everyone felt the same gentle moving of the Holy Spirit.

Afterward, the president of the school stood up and made an amazing statement. He offered financial help to any needy student who wanted to go to New York to work with us on the streets. Those who were interested were to meet me in the school library.

When I got to the library a few minutes later, seventy young people were standing in line!

Out of these seventy, I knew we could use only twenty workers. So I really went to work painting a dark picture. I promised them no money. They would even have to pay their own way to New York. All we could give them was a place to stay and food to eat. I stressed that they were going to risk their lives. I told them about some of our boys who were beaten on the streets. Then I told them there would be lots of other work involved, doing dishes and scrubbing floors and getting the home ready.

To my surprise, we eliminated only twenty.

Now I left the choice to the faculty at the school. By the time I left Springfield, we had chosen sixteen young men and women to come to New York as workers. Four more were chosen from Lee College in Tennessee. One by one, a few weeks later, they began to arrive. They came carrying their suitcases and craning their necks. They were all a little frightened, I think, at the strange new sights of New York, and were wondering what they had gotten into. Here are extracts from a letter written by one of our girls shortly after she arrived:

My dearest family:

Greetings from New York City! I arrived in the Great City at eight fifteen last night. The place was full of people, but God helped me. Teen Challenge wasn't listed in the phone book, but I found out the number and someone came with a car and all my friends came right after me. I had no trouble on the way. None of my buses were late. From Chicago to New York we stopped for three meals and two stops, so it was comfortable.

My job and plans here are as follows:

1. Personal evangelism among girls.
    Monday—Free to do as I wish.
    Tuesday—Street evangelism and street services.
    Wednesday—Hospital visitations to teenage girls.
    Thursday—Jail visits to girls.
    Friday—Street evangelism and street services.
    Saturday—Work with denominational churches.
    Sunday—Work with Pentecostal churches.
2. In charge of girls as dorm counselor. See that the rooms are clean and homework done, etc.
3. In charge as music director.

We are praying for a person to pioneer the girls' evangelism with me.

There were three murders in Joe's section this week.

I must go help cook supper. Don't forget to go to church. I love you.

I'll never forget the evening when I was finally able to say to Gwen, "Honey, we're open for business."

We were standing in the chapel of the center. This room had at one time been the formal drawing room of the old house, and there was a large fireplace against one wall. A richly carved mantel stuck out into the room, and as I talked to Gwen, I leaned up against this mantel.

I reminded her of the evening a year and a half earlier, when I'd stood in the moonlit churchyard in Philipsburg,

watching the wheat wave in the breeze. Now the Lord had brought us to the harvest field. He had given us the tools: twenty fine workers and a belief in the power of the Holy Spirit to change lives.

"Darling," said Gwen, "look!" She pointed to the mantel.

Beautifully carved into the fireplace in our chapel was the bas-relief of a sheaf of wheat, brought in, tied, and harvested.

16

As soon as we got our workers settled, I took them into the chapel and, standing before the bas-relief of the harvested wheat, I gave them a briefing on the makeup of a New York fighting gang.

"*Violence* is the key word to remember about these gangs," I told the young workers. "It can express itself directly in street wars or indirectly through drug addiction or criminal behavior. These ugly things are the rule, not the exception, among the jitterbugging gangs in New York."

It was important for our young workers to know the reason for this pathetic state. "We preachers speak of *lost* sinners. As I got to know these gang members, I couldn't escape the feeling that they were literally acting as if they were lost. They wandered around, looking furtively over their shoulders. They carried weapons, ready at a moment's notice to run or to fight for their lives. These lost boys group together for protection, and there you have the making of a gang."

Virtually without exception these boys had no real home.

Their slang words for home were *prison* and *horror house*. I wanted our workers to know this situation from personal experience, so I took a few of them into the home of one of the street boys I knew.

When we arrived, the door was open; no one was at home.

"You can see why they call it a horror house," whispered a young worker from a Missouri farm. It was true. A family of five lived in this single room. There was no running water, no refrigeration, no stove except for the single-burner hot plate with its frayed wire that sat on a chest of drawers. Down the hall in a single, stinking stall was a toilet and a faucet that served eight families on the floor. The ventilation in the apartment was poor, and a strong odor of gas hung in the air. The room's one window looked out onto a blank brick wall, eight inches away. For light, the family had a single forty-watt bulb that hung naked from the center of the ceiling.

"Why doesn't the family just move?" another young worker asked. "Can't they get into one of the housing projects?"

To answer this question, we got in the car and drove a mile away to a great complex of apartments. These projects, many people thought, were the answer to New York's slums. Bulldozers moved into an overcrowded area, like the one we had just visited. They tore down the old tenements and built towering new buildings in their place.

Now there was a completely uprooted neighborhood. Everybody in it was *lost*. None of the old institutions were left, none of the older and more stable population of professional workers, and none of the known neighbors.

The project we visited was a few years old but already showed serious signs of disintegration. Lawns had long ago been abandoned. Windows on the ground floor were broken and unrepaired. There was obscene writing on the walls. The halls smelled of urine and cheap wine.

We visited a family there I knew. The mother was drunk. Dirty dishes lay on the kitchen table. The boy we had come to visit sat on a torn hassock staring, never speaking.

Once we were outside again, I said, "Usually that boy is out on the streets. Thrown out. He can only come home when his mother has passed out, drunk."

This, I pointed out again, was the making of a teenage fighting gang. Lump a thousand tortured families together in a single neighborhood, and you have a population of teenagers who are hostile and afraid, who flock together looking for security and a sense of belonging. They will create a home for themselves by fighting for a turf that is theirs and that no stranger can violate. This is their fortress.

Many of these boys are degradingly poor. I met one fourteen-year-old who had not eaten a real meal in two days. His grandmother, who took care of him, gave him some change each morning and chased him out of the house. For breakfast he had a Coke, for lunch a hot dog from a street vendor, and for supper he laughed and said he was going on a diet. All evening he nibbled on penny candy.

Strangely, although the boys I met never seemed to have enough money for food, they always had enough for a bottle of wine.

"It really frightens me to see how much drinking these young people do," I said to our workers. "Many of the street boys drink wine all day long. They are seldom really drunk nor are they sober. They start drinking as soon as they meet, at ten or eleven in the morning, and continue until the money runs out."

When we got back to the center, I took our workers into the chapel again and told them the story of Martin Ilensky. Martin was a high school senior who worked part-time to help support his invalid mother. One day when he was not working he went to a vodka party at the horror house of another high school boy. Ten teenagers were there, six boys and four girls. After an hour of drinking, the vodka ran out. The boys took a collection for beer, but Martin refused. A fight followed. A twelve-inch sword appeared from one of the boys' waistbands. There was a swift jab, and Martin Ilensky lay dead on the kitchen floor.

"Now then . . ." I knew the words I was about to say would bother some of our workers, fresh from the seminary. "Suppose you could have talked to Martin Ilensky on some street corner for a few minutes. Remember: It is his fate to die if he goes to that party. What would your first words to him be?"

"I'd tell him that Jesus saves," piped up one boy.

"That's what I was afraid of."

Young eyes looked up, puzzled.

"We've got to be very careful," I said, "that we don't become parrots. I try to keep my ear tuned for phrases—religious terms—that I've heard before. Then when I'm on the street I never use such a phrase without first saying a prayer that I can give it all the power it had when it was spoken for the very first time.

"What," I said, "do you really mean when you say 'Jesus saves'?"

Of course these boys and girls knew the answer to that—

they weren't just mouthing often-heard answers now; they were talking about something that had happened to them.

"It means," said one girl, "that you're born again."

Still, the words didn't have that ring of freshness we had to capture if we were going to touch Martin Ilensky before he was stabbed to death.

"What happened to you when you were born again?" I asked this girl.

The young lady hesitated a moment before she answered. In a voice that caught the attention of the entire room she told about a change that had come into her life one day. She talked of how she had been lonesome and afraid, and of how her life didn't seem to be going anywhere.

"I'd heard about Christ," she said, "but the name was just a word. Then one day a friend told me that Christ could take away my lonesomeness and my fear. We went to church together. The preacher invited me to come forward, and I did. I knelt down in front of everybody and asked this 'Christ,' who had just been a name, to work a change in my life. Nothing has been the same since then," she said. "I really am a new person, which is why they say you're 'born again,' I suppose."

"You lost your lonesomeness?"

"Yes. Altogether."

"What about your fear?"

"That, too."

"Christ is more to you now than just an empty word?"

"Yes. A word can't change things."

The room was silent. "Nor could empty words have changed things for Martin," I said. "Keep this boy in mind when you go out onto the street tomorrow."

By late spring 1961, the Teen Challenge Center was in full operation. Every day—even on Mondays when they were supposed to be off—our young workers were out on the streets of Brooklyn and Harlem and the Bronx, looking for teenagers who needed them. They went to hospitals and jails, to schools and courts. They held street meetings in Greenwich Village and in Coney Island and in Central Park. And as they worked, the flow of kids coming through our center grew from a trickle to a flood. During the first month of operation, the lives of more than five hundred boys and girls had been radically changed; they left the gangs; they sought jobs; they started going to church.

Of this five hundred, perhaps a hundred came to the center for special counseling. Of this hundred, a handful were in such trouble that they needed to live with us at the center, absorbing directly its atmosphere of love.

As the summer wore on and more boys passed through the center, we began to face a moral problem. At one time or another, all of our boys had broken the law. What should they do about that?

It was not a simple question to answer. It would be relatively easy for a boy who had become strong in his new life to take his punishment in jail. But to become strong takes time. There are many crises to pass, many dry periods to ride out, much to learn about the art of being a Christian. If a boy confesses to the police too early and is put in jail, isn't there the risk of losing him? On the other hand, when he has offended society's law, it will hold him back spiritually if he harbors guilt.

I have come to feel that there is no answer that will cover all cases. Often I am puzzled as to what recommendation to make. Pedro, for example, had been living in the center for several days when he came to me complaining, "I can't eat. I can't sleep. I can't sleep at all."

"Why, Pedro?"

"I feel the weight of all my crimes. I have to go to the police and confess."

I listened to him and came to the conclusion that he really did have to confess to the police. Pedro didn't detail his crimes for me because he had too much trouble with English and I could speak very little Spanish.

So I contacted my old friend, Vincente Ortez, to interpret, and together we took Pedro down to the police. The sergeant behind the desk looked up and said, "Yes?"

"I'm Reverend Wilkerson, director of Teen-Age Evangelism," I said. "I have a boy here who was a member of the Dragon gang, and he has some things he wants to confess."

The sergeant asked me to repeat that. When I did, he put down his pencil. "Reverend, we have people coming in all the time to confess things they never did. But if you think the boy's in his right mind, take him upstairs to the detectives' room."

So we went upstairs and waited. Pedro seemed composed. Soon a detective came in and asked me right away if I had forced Pedro to come.

"No," I said. "He's here of his own accord."

"You realize he might go to jail."

I asked Vincente Ortez to explain this to Pedro in Spanish. The boy nodded his head. Yes, he understood.

The detective got paper and pencil and settled back. "All right, Pedro. Suppose you tell us what you want to confess."

"Well," said Pedro, through Vincente Ortez, "do you remember that stabbing . . . ?" and he proceeded to describe a knifing that had taken place in Central Park two months earlier. The detective put his pencil down and called in another officer. They remembered the incident, and their interest picked up considerably. Pedro detailed the events that led up to the knifing. He was on drugs and he needed a fix. He was with two other boys. They spotted a young man sitting by himself on a bench, circled him, robbed him, and then put a knife in his stomach.

Pedro then went on to confess two robberies. The detectives kept him there from six o'clock until twelve o'clock, checking and rechecking facts. They found the boy who had been stabbed, but he had a record and wouldn't press charges. The store Pedro robbed twice also refused to press charges.

In the end the police couldn't find anyone to press charges, and they released Pedro into our custody. We went back to the center, and the next morning, Pedro was up before anyone. He woke the entire house by singing at the top of his lungs, and he greeted everyone with such cheeriness that we couldn't complain. Pedro was a different boy. His heart was filled with a truly amazing joy.

17

As the thermometer on our back porch mounted higher with the summer heat, our twenty workers were busy from early morning until late at night. This was the schedule for the day:

Rising bell at 7:00

Breakfast at 7:30

Dishes and cleanup

Personal devotions until 9:30

Group chapel from 9:30 to 11:30

Dinner at 12:00

Dishes

Prayer

Street work from 2:00 to 6:00, eating sack suppers together on the street

More street work until 7:30

Back to the center for evening services until midnight

Bed

Over the months we built up a cadre of experts in specialized fields who ran the center together. Howard Culver became our administrator. He saw to it that discipline was maintained. This was not always an easy task with twenty lively young collegians and an ever-changing number of young gang members on his hands. Howard's wife, Barbara, was a registered nurse. Her presence was so important for undernourished youngsters and especially with addicts whose bodies go through horrible withdrawal.

If I had a special place in my heart for the next member of our staff, I think it is understandable. He was Nicky. What a day it was for me when Nicky walked shyly through the front door of the center with a beautiful girl on his arm!

"Davie," said Nicky, "I want you to meet my wife, Gloria."

Nicky and Gloria met on the West Coast while they were both in Bible school. I rushed forward to greet them, wringing Nicky's hand and slapping him on the back, and welcoming Gloria so warmly she was a little startled.

Nicky, Gloria and I sat in the office and talked. This was the same boy who had threatened to kill me just three years earlier! At our first encounter, Nicky had impressed me as a hopeless case. Yet here he was, sitting before me a new person—a licensed minister, bursting with plans for the future.

"What I want, Davie," he said, eagerly, "is to work not just with kids, but with the parents. What's the good helping a boy if he's got to go home to a miserable family situation?" It made sense.

Gloria wanted to work at the center, too. She loved children, and when Nicky told her about the eight-, nine- and ten-year-olds who ran on the periphery of the gangs, Gloria pointed out that reaching these kids *before* they got into serious trouble was even better than trying to pull them out of trouble later.

We came at the problems of the street kids from all angles. I was working with the boys, Nicky with the parents, Gloria with the younger kids. But there was one large gap: We had no one whose special interest was in the Debs.

The role of the teenage girl had been growing in importance in the makeup of the gangs. She was known as a Deb. She grouped together with other girls to form auxiliaries to the boy-gangs. Often these girl-gangs took names echoing the names of their male counterpart, as in the Cobras and the Cobrettes.

The girls, I quickly discovered, were often the cause of trouble on the streets. I knew of one rumble that started because a Deb from one gang complained that a boy from a rival gang made a pass at her. Later the girl confessed that she was lying; she made up the story so there would be a fight.

What we needed was a girl on the staff with a strong faith who could gain the Debs' respect and not be shaken by their taunting.

And we found her. Her name was Linda Meisner. She came from a farm in Iowa, and I hoped the city girls wouldn't frighten her.

Linda's job with the Debs was not an easy one. She got her introduction to the girls on her very first Saturday night at the center. Five girls walked through the door and demanded to be shown around. I could smell alcohol on the girls' breath.

"We have a service here at 7:30," I said. "Come then; you'll be welcome." The girls came back at 7:30, bringing a group of boys with them.

The girls giggled, mocked, blew loud bubbles with their gum, got up and walked in and out. Several of the girls got out knives and started cutting their shoelaces. In the middle of my sermon, they began to argue with me from the floor of the little chapel. I turned the meeting over to an all-girl trio (which included Linda), but they couldn't sing above the noise.

Finally we just gave up trying to hold an orderly meeting and turned our attention instead to individual boys and girls. Most of the girls got out of their seats and stormed out the door, slamming it loudly.

The evening broke up early. This was Linda's introduction to her future friends.

"It's hopeless," said Linda the next morning. "I don't see how I can work with kids as hard as these."

"Wait till you see what the Holy Spirit can do, Linda, before you make up your mind."

The very next Tuesday, Linda had her first experience of watching the change. Afterward, she showed me the letter she had written to her parents:

> . . . *every* minute is full of excitement and a new adventure. On Tuesday the entire gang of boys and girls returned. We wanted to have them come on different nights, but the girls begged to come in with the boys for a service. They promised not to laugh and to be good; so we let them all in. During the service, we sang "Jesus Breaks Every Fetter." Dave asked if there was anything that anyone would like

for God to break in their lives. A fourteen-year-old girl said she would like to be delivered from heavy drinking every night. One of the girls pulled up her sleeve and asked if God could forgive this—a line showing heroin inserts. The girls behaved as well as I've seen girls behave anywhere.

From that moment on, girls from the gangs sought Linda out for help. Elaine, for instance, one of the girls from the local gang, came to Linda with a very common problem for a Deb; she was poisoning her life with hate. Elaine was a hard girl; you could feel the hatred that clung about her. She was a discipline problem at school and at home. If she was told to sit, she'd stand; if told to stand, she'd sit. If she was told she had to stay in, she'd slip out; or if she was told to get out of the house, nothing could make her leave.

One afternoon Elaine came to see Linda. They sat in the kitchen and talked. Elaine's first words were that she had been drinking heavily. Then she told Linda that she had recently started going to wild parties, and they were getting wilder.

Suddenly, Elaine began to cry. "Linda," she said, "I don't want to hate myself anymore. Can you help me?"

Soon Elaine was coming regularly to our gang church meetings that we held every Wednesday night. She stood up and told what happened to her hate. Her face was open and fresh and free as Linda's. She started bringing her cousins and her friends. She stopped her drinking and her wild partying.

Elaine was no isolated case. Day in and day out, we could count on reaching girls like Elaine with this special kind of love. I'll never forget the day Elaine put her finger on the quality of the love that redeems.

"I've finally got it figured out, Reverend Wilkerson," she said. "Christ's love is a love with no strings attached."

Elaine was right. Christ's love is a love that asks nothing in return. It is a love that wants only the *best* for these boys and girls.

In one of her letters home, Linda wrote that her life was in constant danger. This was not an exaggeration. We did what we could to protect our workers. For instance, we had a rule that street work must be done in teams of two or three. We had a rule that girls were not allowed to make contact with boys on the street, and boys were not allowed to make contact with girls. And we had a rule that workers must make contact with each other at regular intervals, especially at night.

The fact remained, however, that our young students were walking into areas where even armed policemen traveled in pairs for protection. Many of the teenagers on the street carried concealed weapons. If a boy was high on heroin, he might lash out with his knife, just for kicks. But a much more serious problem was the jealousy that was aroused when our workers threatened to break up relationships.

One night Linda and a partner, Kay, were out near midnight on a sweltering summer night. The girls should have gone to bed, but they headed out into the night, praying that the Holy Spirit would lead them to girls in need.

They came to a store, and looking inside, they saw four

teenage girls listening to music and sipping Cokes. Linda and Kay walked in and struck up a conversation with the girls. The four girls argued for only a few moments, then one of them began to cry.

"Come on," said another of the foursome. "Let's go out on the street. I don't want anyone to hear this."

So all the girls stepped outside. Hardly had they started talking again when all *four* of the girls started to cry.

Two fellows walked up.

"What's going on?" they asked.

The teenage girls told them they didn't want to talk to the boys.

This aroused the boys' curiosity even more than the tears, and they pressed in. "What are you trying to do?" they asked Linda. "Take our girls away from us?"

One of the boys began to pinch Linda. "Come over into the park, and I'll show you something." The other fellow joined in, and the two of them made suggestions to Linda and Kay that left them embarrassed.

But looking the leader of the boys squarely in the eye, Linda said slowly, "God bless you."

The boy's jaw dropped. Linda turned and picked up her conversations with the four girls. The boys sputtered a while, then one of them said, "Let's get out of here."

Linda and Kay went back to their talks with the teenage girls. After a while, they became aware that a whole crowd of boys was descending slowly on them from many different directions.

"Watch out," whispered one of the girls.

Linda and Kay moved closer together, but they continued talking calmly. Suddenly there was a loud laugh and

a cry. All of the girls were surrounded by yelping, shouting teenage boys who crowded in and separated Linda and Kay from the other girls.

"You make me mad," said the leader of the boys. "You talking religion to our girls? You'll take them away from us."

Again Linda and Kay heard language they'd never heard before. The boys pushed and taunted them.

Something glistened in the dark. One of the boys held a knife in his hand that shone in the night.

Without warning he lunged at Linda. She slipped her body sideways. The knife slashed through her clothing. It ripped out a chunk of her dress, but it did not touch her body.

Linda turned to the boy while he was still off balance. Once again she spoke the words that had helped her before. Her voice was low as she said, "God bless you."

She took Kay by the arm. "Come over to the center tomorrow: 416 Clinton Avenue," she said. "We'll be expecting you." Then she and Kay sauntered off across the street.

At first the boys followed them. Then the leader shouted for the boys to stop. "Forget it," he said. "I don't feel like fooling with them."

Linda and Kay came back to the center shaking. But the next day they picked up conversations with the four girls, and the next night Linda and Kay were out on the street again.

18

The center turned out to be what we hoped it would be: a home. Full of love, subject to spiritual discipline, heading toward the same common goal, but free. There was a release in that kind of atmosphere that could not be overestimated. It kept us from becoming tied up in knots. It allowed us to laugh.

I was glad about that. It didn't seem likely to me that any true house of God would be a drab and somber place. Certainly the center was no place for the long-of-face. If it wasn't a pillow fight in the girls' dorm, or a short sheet in the boys', then it was sugar in the saltshaker. But we kept our young people so busy that there wasn't much energy left for roughhousing.

It surprised me to discover how much of the free give-and-take we encountered at 416 Clinton Avenue centered on the kitchen.

I think maybe God saw to it, during those first long months of our work at the center, that we never found a cook. We tried every system under the sun to keep ourselves fed, but the one that never worked out was to have a full-time cook. A kitchen is the heart of a home, and a cook has a way of chasing you out so that she can get her work done. Thus you are chased from the heart of the home.

Not so with the center, because we could never come up with a cook.

The result was a wonderful, chaotic, happy mess. To understand it you must first understand where the food itself came from. Like everything else at the center, we got our food by praying for it. Each day we prayed for food, and the way it came in was a vivid lesson to young people—including live-in gang members—learning about faith. People sent in a ham, potato chips, fruit, vegetables. Or they sent in money not earmarked for a special purpose.

One day, however, the kids went down to breakfast, and there wasn't anything on the table. By the time I arrived, the center was buzzing with the problem of no food.

"Your prayers didn't work I guess this time, did they, Dave?" said one of the gang boys.

Lord, I said to myself, *teach us a lesson in faith that will live with us forever.* Aloud, I said, "Let's make an experiment. Here we are without food for the day, right?"

The boy nodded his head.

"The Bible says, 'Give us this day our daily bread,' right? So why don't we all go into the chapel right now and pray that we either get the food for this day or money to buy the food."

"Before lunch, Dave?" said the boy. "I'm getting hungry."

"Before lunch. How many do we have here?" I glanced around. The number in the center was constantly shifting. On that day we could count 25 people who would need to be fed. I figured it would cost between 30 and 35 dollars to feed that number of people lunch and supper. Others agreed. So we went into the chapel, closed the door, and began to pray.

"While You're at it, Lord," said the gang boy, "would You please see that we don't go hungry for the rest of the summer?"

I thought this was stretching things a bit. But I had to admit that it would leave us freer to work at other kinds of prayer if we didn't have to pay so much attention to such basic needs as food.

One of the things about our prayer at the center was that it tended to be a bit loud. If we felt concerned, we said so not only with our lips but with the tone of our prayer.

And this morning we were quite concerned. While we were saying so in tones that left no doubt about how we felt, a stranger walked in.

We didn't even hear when she knocked on the door of the chapel. When finally she opened the door and saw all 25 of us on our knees, thanking God for the food He had given us in the past and thanking Him, too, for the food He would be giving us, somehow, in this emergency, I'm sure she was sorry she had come.

"Excuse me," she said.

I immediately got up. The rest kept right on with their prayer.

This lady started asking questions. I noticed that the more she found out about what we were doing, the more enthusiastic she became. Finally, she asked about the prayer session. I told her about realizing that we had no food in the house and about the purpose of the prayer.

"When did you begin this prayer?" the lady asked.

"About an hour ago."

"Well," she said, "that is truly extraordinary. I knew very little about your work. But an hour ago I received a sudden impulse to do something completely out of character for me. I felt that I was supposed to empty my piggy bank and bring the contents to you. Now I know the reason." She reached into her purse.

She placed a white envelope on my desk and with an expression of hope that it would be of some help, she thanked me for showing her our center and left. That envelope contained just over 32 dollars, the amount we needed to feed ourselves for the rest of the day.

And that teenager's prayer was answered, too! For the rest of the summer, we never again wanted for food.

Finding enough money to run the center was a matter of even greater difficulty. As the time grew closer for our young workers to go back to school, we made a reckoning of what it had cost us to run the center full swing for the summer. We were astonished at how much cash was involved.

There were monthly electric bills and food bills, printing bills and transportation bills. There were clothing bills for our street boys, whose clothes we often had to throw away; there were repair bills and plumbing bills and taxes. There were salaries. Even those small wages paid to staff added up. Our expenses regularly ran more than a thousand dollars each week.

We never had more than a few dollars in the bank. As fast as the money came in, we found a need for it. Often

I yearned for a financial situation that would allow us to breathe a little more easily. But just as often, I came back to the conviction that the Lord wanted us to live this way—to depend totally on God for the needs of His work.

Where did the weekly money come from? A lot of it was raised by teenagers themselves. All across the country young boys and girls helped support this work by babysitting, mowing lawns and washing cars. Individual churches took us as a missionary concern.

We were usually able to handle weekly expenses. But we were faced with a crisis come summer's end. In two weeks the second mortgage on the home was due: fifteen thousand dollars. I had not put anything aside toward its payment. We were barely scraping by as it was.

August 28, 1961, was our deadline. We would have to face reality on that date.

19

Late one afternoon Maria telephoned me to say that she wanted to see me. I called Linda in and briefed her. "This is a girl you should know," I said. "She has tremendous potential if her energies can ever be channeled in the right direction. She's brave; but it's gang bravery. When she became president of her gang, she had to stand with her back to the wall and let the kids hit her as hard as they could. She's a brilliant organizer, but she's thrown this away on the gang. She built her unit up until it had more than three hundred girls in it.

"But I think she's coming because she's back on heroin."

I briefed Linda on Maria's battle with the drug. I told her how she'd been a mainline addict when I first met her nearly four years earlier. I told how she'd tried to throw the habit after she came forward at St. Nick's, how she'd married, how everything seemed to go smoothly for a while. Maria quit the gang, her husband got a job, children began to come along.

But one day Maria and Johnny had a fight. The first thing

Maria did was connect with a seller and start "drilling" again. She had gone off once more for a short while. But now, I felt sure, she was calling to say she was back on again.

When Maria arrived, what a tragic change had come over her since I last saw her! Her eyes were glassy. Her nose ran. Her complexion was pasty. Her hair was matted and unkempt. But what struck me the most about Maria were her hands. She held them in tight fists. She kept clenching and unclenching those fists.

"Reverend Wilkerson," she said, "I need help."

"Come on in, Maria," I said. We pulled up a chair for her. "I've told Linda about you, Maria. Everything, both good and bad. I want you to get to know Linda. She's working with a lot of girls around the city. She's got a real way of understanding. You'll get along."

Maria and Linda did have their talk. Later Linda came into my office, worried that she had not gotten through at all to the girl.

"It's the drugs, Dave," she said. "It's death on the installment plan."

A few days later, matters got worse. Maria phoned Linda, pleading for help. She was about to get into serious trouble, she said, and she didn't know how to stop herself. She had just taken heroin and had drunk a full bottle of whiskey, and she and her old gang were heading off to fight a rival gang. "We're going to kill a girl named Dixie," Maria said. "You've got to stop us."

Linda and two of her partners raced uptown. They barged right into the headquarters of the girls' gang. They stayed for more than an hour, and before they left, the fight was called off.

"Dave," said Linda when she got back, "this thing is desperate. We've simply got to do something for these girls."

What is this thing called drug addiction?

Most narcotics addicts are lonesome, frustrated, angry, and usually come from a broken home. One sampling of drugs and the boy discovers what it would be like to be permanently happy. He forgets his drunken father and wandering mother, the stifling poverty, and the total lack of love in his life. He is free, and that is no small thing.

Now comes the truly fiendish part of this story.

Heroin costs money—every day. How does an addict pay for drugs?

He might turn to crime. Muggings, purse snatchings, shoplifting, housebreaking, armed robbery and auto thefts became a major problem in New York. The police said the reason was drug addiction.

Shorty was nineteen years of age and addicted to heroin. He had been on drugs since he was fifteen years old. Tammy was Shorty's girlfriend, a very beautiful girl of seventeen.

Shorty asked me to "get Tammy off the stuff," and I agreed to see the girl. When Shorty and I tapped on the door of a dark, rat-infested basement room in Brooklyn, there was a quick shuffling inside. We waited, while an impatient Shorty mumbled under his breath. When the door opened, there stood Tammy, openmouthed in surprise at our visit.

There were two other young men in the dimly lit room; they had rolled up the sleeves on their left arms. On the table before them lay a needle, a bottle cap "cooker," a glass of water, and a small cellophane bag containing a white substance: heroin.

"Who's he?" said Tammy, jerking her head toward me.

"He's okay," said Shorty. "He's a preacher. I asked him here."

Tammy turned her back on us and went ahead with the heating process we had interrupted.

Shorty turned to me and whispered, "Don't try to stop them, Preach. If you mess up the fix, they'll kill you. I mean that. If you go out and try to get the cops, we'll be gone by the time you get back. Stick around. It's good for your education."

So I stuck around and got my education in what it's like to be a teenage addict. I shall never be the same, as a result of the scene I witnessed in the next few moments. The preparation of the fix had taken some time. Now each teenager, including Shorty, pushed and struggled to shoot up first. The sickest was allowed to drill before the others, and Shorty suddenly went into a seizure of shaking and retching and moaning—I suppose so that he could be first. The four youngsters watched one of the boys pour heroin into the cap cooker.

With shaking hands the boy lit two matches under the cooker and boiled the contents. The other addict took off his belt and applied a tourniquet to Shorty's arm. The others were getting very agitated. They stood by gritting their teeth and clenching their fists to keep from grabbing the loaded needle from Shorty's hand. Tears streamed down their cheeks as they cursed and bit their lips.

Then, one by one, there was that final puncture that was so exhilarating.

I have never felt so close to hell. The kids drifted off into a kind of euphoria.

"What about it, Preach? You going to get Tammy off the stuff?" Shorty asked, suddenly remembering why he had asked me in.

I told him I would certainly try. And I did try to talk with Tammy then and there, but she simply looked at me with glassy eyes. What could I offer that she didn't have right now, she said. She was in heaven. I just didn't know what heaven was like. She could handle herself without any help from me.

Shorty, too, thought better of having invited me in now that he had his fix. When I told him that I had no magic cure, that all I could offer was help while he went cold turkey, he looked at me and said, "Well, what'd you come here for, then?"

So I failed.

I left the apartment. When I went back to try again, Tammy and Shorty had disappeared. Nobody knew where they were. Nor did anybody seem to care.

20

The tremendous hold that drugs have on the human body cannot be explained in physical terms alone. My grandfather would say that the devil had these boys in his grip, and I think my grandfather is right. The boys themselves say this, but in a different way:

"Davie," I was told over and again, "there are two habits you've got to kick if you're hooked. The body habit and the mind habit. The body habit's not too much of a problem: You just stay in sheer hell for three days, put up with a little less torture for another month, and you're free.

"But that mind habit, Davie . . . that's something terrible! There's a thing inside you that *makes* you come back. Something whispering to you. We can't get rid of him, Davie. But you're a preacher. Maybe this Holy Spirit you talk about, maybe He can help."

I don't know why it took so long for me to realize that this was, indeed, the direction we should take. The realization came about as an evolution, starting with a failure and ending with a magnificent discovery.

The failure was a boy named Joe. I'll never forget the four traumatic days I spent with him, trying to bring him through the pain of withdrawing from addiction to heroin.

Joe was such a nice guy. He had not come into his addiction by the usual route. He had been working for a coal company. One day he slipped and fell down a chute. The accident put him in the hospital for several months, and for most of that time Joe was in severe pain. To help relieve his agony, the doctor prescribed a narcotic. By the time Joe was released from the hospital, he was addicted.

"I couldn't get any more of the drug," he told me. "But I discovered that there was a kind of cough syrup that had narcotics in it and I started walking all over the city buying it."

After a while this didn't satisfy Joe's growing need. He knew that some of his old high school buddies were using heroin, and he got in touch with them. From then on the pattern was typical. First sniffing, then skin popping, then mainline injections. When Joe came to us, he was deeply addicted.

"Can you stay here at the center for three or four days?" I asked. "You can live upstairs with the workers."

Joe shrugged.

"It won't be easy, you know. You'll be going off cold turkey."

Joe shrugged again.

Cold turkey—instantaneous withdrawal—was the method we used partly because we had no choice: We could not administer the withdrawal drugs they used in hospitals. But we preferred cold turkey because withdrawal is faster: three days vs. three weeks. The pain is more intense, but it is over sooner.

We brought Joe to the center and gave him a room upstairs with the male workers. Barbara, our registered nurse living at the home, would keep an eye on Joe all the time he was with us. We also put a doctor on alert in case we should need him.

"Joe," I said, as soon as we had him settled in, "as of this moment the withdrawal has started. I can promise you that you won't be alone for one second. When we aren't with you in person, we will be with you in prayer."

We weren't going to take the boy off drugs and leave him alone to suffer. The entire four days would be coupled with intensive, supportive prayer around the clock. Day and night boys and girls would be in the chapel interceding for Joe. Others would be with him in person upstairs reading Scripture to him.

We had Joe learn the 31st Psalm. We call it the Song of the Addict.

> Pull me out of the net that they have laid privily for me: for thou art my strength. (v. 4)

> Have mercy upon me, O Lord, for I am in trouble: mine eye is consumed with grief, yea, my soul and my belly. (v. 9)

> For my life is spent with grief, and my years with sighing: my strength faileth because of mine iniquity, and my bones are consumed. (v. 10)

> I was a reproach among all mine enemies, but especially among my neighbours, and a fear to mine acquaintance: they that did see me without fled from me. (v. 11)

I am forgotten as a dead man out of mind: I am like a broken vessel. (v. 12)

Once the withdrawal pains began, Joe sweated through the symptoms. Barbara checked his condition regularly. I hated to go into his room. Joe lay on the bed gripping his stomach as the cramps hit him again and again. His body was a high pink. Sweat poured off him, leaving the mattress soaked. He cried out in his pain and pounded his head with his hands. He wanted water, then threw it up. All I could do was hold his hand and promise him that we cared.

At night we set up a tape recorder by Joe's bed and played Scripture readings to him. I stayed at the center during this. Often during the night I would slip into the chapel to be sure someone was there, then up the stairs to see how Joe was doing. The recorder was softly repeating portions of the Bible to the boy as he tossed in fitful sleep. Never once during those three days and nights did the torment let up. It was a terror to watch.

Then, on the fourth day, Joe seemed better.

He walked around the center smiling wanly and saying that he thought maybe the worst was over. All of us were happy with him. When Joe said he wanted to go home to see his parents, I was a little dubious, but there was nothing we could do to detain the boy if he wanted to leave.

So, smiling and thankful, Joe walked out the front door and turned down Clinton Avenue.

The next morning we learned that Joe had been arrested for robbery and possession of narcotics.

"What went wrong?" I asked at a staff meeting. "The boy got all the way through the worst three days he would ever have to spend. He had a tremendous investment to protect. And he threw it all away."

"Why don't you talk to the boys who have come off successfully?" said Howard Culver.

There were several such boys. One by one I called them in and listened to their stories of deliverance. They all spoke of a common experience.

I spoke to Nicky and asked him when it was that he felt he had victory over his old way of life. Something tremendous had happened to him, he said, at the time of his conversion on the street corner. He had been introduced at that time to the love of God. But it wasn't until later that he knew he had complete victory.

"When was that, Nicky?"

"At the time of my baptism in the Holy Spirit."

I called in others and asked the same thing. Again and again I got the same report.

A pattern was emerging. I felt I was on the verge of something tremendous.

21

Shortly after we became interested in the Holy Spirit's role in helping a boy rid himself of an addiction to narcotics, we had a visit at the center from a Jesuit priest. He, too, wanted to know more about the baptism. He had heard our young people at a street rally and was so impressed that he wanted to know their secret.

We spent an afternoon with Father Gary at the center. The first thing we did was show him the references to the experience in the Bible. "The baptism of the Holy Spirit is not a denominational experience," I said. "We have Episcopalians and Lutherans and Baptists and Methodists working with us, all of whom have been filled with the Holy Spirit."

In its essence, we told Father Gary, the baptism is a religious experience that gives you power. "But you will receive power when the Holy Spirit comes upon you," said Jesus when He showed Himself to His apostles after His death.

Father Gary and I bent over the Bible. "The first reference to this special experience comes in the early part of

the Gospel story. The Jews, you remember, wondered for a while if John the Baptist was the Messiah. But John told them, 'There cometh one mightier than I after me, the latchet of whose shoes I am not worthy to stoop down and unloose. I indeed have baptized you with water: but he shall baptize you with the Holy Ghost'" (Mark 1:7–8).

From the beginning of Christianity, then, this baptism of the Holy Ghost has had a special significance because it marks the difference between the mission of a believer, no matter how bold and effective, and the mission of Christ: Jesus would baptize His followers with the Holy Ghost. In His last hours on earth, Jesus spent a great deal of time talking to His disciples about the Holy Ghost, who would come after His death to stand by them, comfort them, lead them, and give them power that would allow them to carry His mission forward.

Then, after the crucifixion, He appeared to them and told them not to leave Jerusalem. "You must wait," He said, "for the promise made by my Father, about which you have heard me speak: John, as you know, baptized with water, but you will be baptized with the Holy Spirit, and within the next few days . . . you will receive power when the Holy Spirit comes upon you" (Acts 1:4–5, 8, NEB).

We continued to the second chapter of Acts. "It was immediately after this," I reminded Father Gary, "that the disciples were gathered together in Jerusalem to celebrate Pentecost. 'While the day of Pentecost was running its course they were all together in one place, when suddenly there came from the sky a noise like that of a strong driving wind, which filled the whole house where they were sitting. And there appeared to them tongues like flames of fire, dispersed among them and resting on each one. And they were all filled with the Holy Spirit and began to talk in other tongues, as the Spirit gave them power of utterance.'"

"A vast change took place in the apostles after this experience at Pentecost. Before, they had been powerless. Afterward, they received that power Christ spoke about. They healed the sick, cast out demons, raised the dead. The same men who had hidden during the crucifixion went on after this experience to stand up to the world with their message."

I told Father Gary about the gigantic revival that swept the United States, Canada, England and South America in the early 1900s. At the heart of this revival was the message that the power given to the Church at Pentecost had for the most part fallen away but could be brought back through the baptism of the Holy Spirit. "The book of Acts tells of five different times when people received this experience," I said, "and the early Pentecostals noticed that in four out of five of these times, the people who were baptized with the Holy Spirit began to 'speak in other tongues.'"

Father Gary wanted to know what speaking in other tongues was like. "It's like talking in another language. A language you don't understand." I pointed out the places in the Bible where this experience followed the baptism of the Holy Spirit. The disciples spoke in tongues at Pentecost; Saul was filled with the Holy Spirit after his Damascus Road conversion and subsequently spoke in tongues, saying, "I thank my God, I speak with tongues more than ye all" (1 Corinthians 14:18). The members of Cornelius's household were baptized with the Holy Spirit and began to speak in tongues. The new Christians at Ephesus were similarly baptized and began to speak in tongues.

Father Gary wanted to know what the actual experience was like.

"Why don't you ask the kids?" I said. We invited him to have lunch with us, and there Father Gary listened as several of our young people described what it had been like when they were filled with the Spirit.

The first was a girl named Neda. We had found her on Coney Island, wandering around as if lost. "I used to drink a lot," she said now, "and I hated my parents, especially my mother. I came here to the center and sat in the chapel and listened to the other kids talk about how Jesus helped them. 'We still get tempted,' they said, 'but now we run into the chapel and pray.' When they prayed, they spoke in another language but they looked happy and sure of themselves. When they were done, their temptation was gone.

"So they made me want the same thing. I went into the chapel one day to pray by myself. I started telling God all about my problems and I asked Him to come into my life like He had to those drug addicts. Something took over my speech. It made me feel like I was sitting down by a river that somehow was flowing through me and bubbled up out of me like a musical language. After that one of the workers showed me in the book of Acts what it was all about. It was the most wonderful thing that ever happened."

The next boy spoke. "First of all," said John, "I know this is real. And you know how? Because afterward Jesus Christ seemed to come right out of the Bible. He became a living person who wanted to stand with me through my problems."

"Yes," said Father Gary. "This is wonderful."

"With me," said a boy named Joseph, "He helped me get rid of drugs. I was beginning to skin pop heroin. When I heard about Jesus, it kind of shocked me that He loved people in spite of all their sins. Then I heard that He comes into us with this baptism of the Holy Spirit.

"So I got to wanting this, just like Neda. In the chapel, I cried to God for help, and that's when He came around. I was speaking in a new language. At first I thought I was crazy, but I knew I couldn't be. I wasn't lonely anymore. I didn't want any more drugs. I loved everybody. For the first time in my life I felt clean."

On and on the kids went, each telling what happened to him or her. Father Gary left an hour later. I wish he had stayed a little longer because that same night another boy received the baptism, and he could have witnessed the experience himself.

22

Our hopes were very high now that the baptism would always, and permanently, free boys from the hold of heroin.

There was a good basis for this hope. As soon as we suspected that there was a relationship between the baptism and a boy's ability to throw the habit, we made a special effort to lead our young addicts into the experience.

Time and again we got the same results. Harvey had been referred to us by the courts; he had been deeply addicted to heroin for three years, but after the baptism he said the temptation itself went away.

Johnny had been on heroin for four years and pulled away successfully after his baptism.

Lefty had used the needle for two years, and after his baptism he not only stopped drugs, he decided to go into the ministry.

Vincent used heroin for two years, until his baptism, when he stopped instantaneously.

Ruben had a four-year addiction; at his baptism he was given the power to stop.

Eddie had started on heroin when he was twelve years old; fifteen years later he was still using the drug, and was nearly dead from its continual use. The baptism of the Holy Spirit released him from his addiction.

Then one of the boys slipped. Even after the baptism of the Holy Spirit. He had not learned that *living* in the Spirit is as necessary as *receiving* the Spirit.

Ralph had been on heroin for three years. He tried a hundred times to break the addiction. He tried to leave his gang, where his buddies were mainlining with him. Each time he failed. There was only one way out, Ralph thought: He had to take his own life before he took the life of someone else when he was desperate for a fix. One night, Ralph climbed on a roof. He stood at the ledge, ready to dive headfirst into the street. He was waiting only until the sidewalk below him was clear.

At that moment, he heard singing.

It came from one of our Gang Churches, meeting in a building directly across the street from where Ralph stood. He stepped down from his perch. He listened to the rest of the song, and then he walked down the stairs of the building and crossed the street. A sign outside invited him to come in and hear the story of how God was working in Brooklyn streets to help boys addicted to drugs and tied to the gangs.

He went in. And Ralph was never the same. He turned his life over to Christ, and later he received the baptism of the Spirit.

We were very proud of Ralph. He went off the needle for over a year. He left New York and went out to California to

live, and all that while he was clean. Then, he came back and paid us a visit. He was all right for several days, but I noticed a despondency settle over him whenever he returned to his old neighborhood. I learned that his friends were taunting him about the needle. Ralph was being tempted again.

And then he fell. He made contact, went up to his room, and stuck the needle in his veins.

Five times, before Ralph received the baptism of the Holy Spirit, he had tried to pull off drugs. Each time he was so disgusted with himself after falling that he started to drill more heavily than ever. Now he had been off over a year and was drilling again.

But a strange thing happened this time. The shot did not have its usual effect. The next day Ralph crept into the center and asked for me. When he came into my office, he closed the door.

"Something funny's happened, Davie," Ralph said, after he finally found courage to tell me what he had done. "After I got through drilling, it was like I hadn't had anything at all. It wasn't anything like what I'd felt before. I felt something else, though. I suddenly had this strong urge to run to the nearest church and pray. That's what I did. Davie, this time I didn't feel disgusted like before. Instead of going from bad to worse, the temptation went away."

Ralph came back to us humbled and fully aware of the fact that the baptism had made him Christ's in a special way. He couldn't get away from Him even when he tried.

Certainly we could not claim a magical cure for drug addiction. All we could say was that we found a power stronger than narcotics. That power was the Holy Spirit, who, unlike narcotics, captured our boys only to liberate them.

We had much to learn about what this religious experience could and could not do in unhappy lives. Every day we made new discoveries.

One day Linda and I were sitting in my office discussing these things and wondering where they might lead us. I was aware that there was one name neither one of us was mentioning: Maria.

"Do you think Maria could ever receive the baptism?" I asked. I saw in Linda's eyes that she wondered the same thing. Maria had been on heroin for years. The last time she had come in to see us, neither Linda nor I thought she had long to live.

We prayed for a miracle in Maria's life. Both of us nursed the dream of guiding her into the baptism there at the center. But it wasn't to come that way. One day, we got a telephone call from Maria, and she was in Reverend Ortez's church.

"Reverend Wilkerson!" she nearly shouted into the phone. "I got wonderful news! Last night I received the Holy Ghost!" She could hardly talk for excitement, so I asked her to put Reverend Ortez on the phone. He described the event, and I could just see it: Maria walking into the church; Maria working her way through other men and women until she found an empty chair; Maria listening to the preaching and hearing the altar call; Maria going forward. I could even hear her voice, so husky the last time she visited us, now begging the Lord to send His Spirit to dwell in her.

I could see her sink to her knees and feel the hope in her

heart as warm hands were laid on her head. Then the soft, melodic, bubbling language that she did not understand, coming from her own throat, the sign that prayer had been answered. Reverend Ortez was jubilant. "We've all waited a long time for this, haven't we?" he said.

"Indeed we have. It's another victory."

Nevertheless, I was filled with apprehension. I knew that when Maria got angry, she went back to the needle.

One evening, late, Maria stepped off a bus on a street in Manhattan, near her old turf. From out of the shadows stepped three girls.

"Hi, Maria."

Maria turned. She recognized the girls as members of the old gang. She greeted them warmly. In the dark behind them, she recognized, too, the form of a boy.

"Say, Maria," one of the girls said, "we hear you're off H. We hear you've got religion now."

"That's right," said Maria.

"Well, now, ain't that just wonderful? You're not having to spend all that money on heroin. I wonder if you'd lend a couple of friends a dollar or two."

Maria knew what the money would go for. Many were the times she had sat in a darkened room with these same girls, twisting a belt around her arm and pumping a syringe full of heroin into her veins.

"I'm sorry," she said. "Not for what you're going to use the money . . ."

Maria never saw the blow coming. A girl's fist plunged into her stomach. Maria doubled over. Her first instinct was to fight back, and Maria had been known all over the area for her fierce fighting. But she stood there, hands at her sides. Like the first day when she passed her test for the presidency of the club, Maria took punishment without resisting, without whimpering.

But this time Maria was praying.

She was praying, too, when the knife went into her side. She was praying while the threesome leaned over her prone body and grabbed her purse and ran, laughing, down the street.

After a while, Maria stood up, slowly. She made her way home somehow. Johnny helped her take off her bloodstained clothes and examined the wound. The knife had pierced her flesh close to the ribs, but the wound wasn't deep, and Johnny didn't think it would be serious.

What he did worry about was Maria's emotions over the incident. What would happen to her now? Far too often he had watched his wife come along the road to recovery, then slip when something made her angry.

But that night, after she had bathed her bruises and put bandages on the knife cut, Maria fell asleep with the peace of a child.

Maria paid us a visit at the center a few days after her beating. She walked in with the black and blue markings of her bruises still livid.

"They messed me up a bit, Reverend Wilkerson. But I prayed and the Holy Spirit was with me."

I looked at Linda, who was as astonished as I at the change. "That's all we need to know," I said.

The next time I saw Maria, she and her family were on their way to Puerto Rico to attend a Spanish training school to equip the couple for full-time work with the church. Johnny stood proudly at Maria's side. Their three young children hung shyly to her freshly starched skirt, and they were clinging to a mother they were beginning to trust. Maria's hair gleamed in the sun, and her hands hung relaxed at her side.

As I watched this family, I found myself repeating the words of Jesus, "Ye shall know the truth, and the truth shall make you free."

23

For most people in Brooklyn, the morning of August 28, 1961, was just another bright, hot summer morning. But not for us at the Teen Challenge Center.

At noon we were supposed to hand over a certified check to the holders of our second mortgage. The amount needed was $15,000.

"How much money do we have in the bank?" I asked Paul DiLena.

"I don't even want to tell you."

"How much?"

"Fourteen dollars."

I had been counting so much on another miracle. Somehow in my heart I had confidence that we weren't going to lose the center, and yet here we were at our deadline and there was no money.

Noon came and went, and still there was no miracle.

I had to ask myself serious questions about my own confidence. Had I expected too much of God without doing enough myself?

I spoke to Julius Fried, our attorney. "Could you arrange for an extension?"

Julius spent the afternoon poring over documents, and when he finished his day's work, he announced that he had succeeded in getting an extension.

"They've agreed to wait until September tenth," Julius said. "But if the money isn't in their hands by that time, they will start foreclosure proceedings. Do you have any ideas?"

"Yes," I said, "I'm going to pray about it." Julius was accustomed to the praying ways of the center, but at that moment I think he wished for a director who was more practical.

That afternoon I did something rash. I called all the young people together, gang members, drug addicts, college boys and girls, staff members, and told them that the center was safe.

There was a great rejoicing. "I think we ought to go into the chapel and thank God," I said.

So we did. We went in, closed the doors, and praised the Lord for having saved this home for His use. Finally someone asked, "Say, David, where'd the money come from?"

"It hasn't come in yet."

Twenty-five frozen smiles.

"But before September tenth," I said, "the money will be in our hands, I'm sure. By that date, I'll have a check for $15,000 to show you. I just thought we ought to thank God ahead of time."

With that I walked out.

September first came. With every passing day, I spent time on the telephone, seeing if I could find the solution to our problem. Every sign pointed to His wanting us to continue our work. The summer had been good. Our records showed that 2,500 young people all over New York had turned their lives over to Christ. Hundreds of boys and girls had poured through the center on their way to new jobs, new outlooks, new lives. Twelve were actually preparing for the ministry.

"It all started with that picture in *Life*," I said to Gwen one night.

"Isn't it strange that you've never been allowed to see those boys from the trial?" she said.

It was strange. I had written, and telephoned, and knocked on doors for nearly four years. But, for reasons beyond my comprehension, I was never allowed to work closely with the very boys whose tragedy had brought me to New York in the first place. Perhaps, when the boys were released from prison, I would be allowed to tell them about the concern that was still on my heart for them.

There was a boy, however, from those very first days in New York, whose life still touched mine: Angelo Morales.

One morning Angelo came to visit us. Together we relived that first day when he bumped into me on the stairs outside Luis Alvarez's father's apartment. Now Angelo himself was about to graduate from seminary. He, too, would be working with me at the center.

"If there *is* a center, Angelo," I said, sharing with him our financial problems.

"Is there anything I can do?" Angelo asked.

"Yes. Get into the chapel with the others and pray. While you are praying, we'll be on the phone."

Every member of our board was busy making telephone calls to old friends of the center. Help came in, but never in the quantity needed to meet the $15,000 note on September tenth.

Among the telephone calls was one to Clem Stone's office in Chicago. Harald Bredesen placed it, admitting openly that he was a little embarrassed. Clem had already been more than generous with the center. We tried to keep him in close touch with the progress of our work at all times, not just when we needed money, but I suspect that when Clem heard a call was coming from the Teen Challenge Center, his natural instinct would be to place a protective hand over his wallet.

It was Clem's son whom Harald reached on the telephone, September eighth. They had a long talk. Harald told about the work that had been accomplished already, and he thanked the Stones for their part in that. Then he got to the point.

"We've got to have $15,000 by day after tomorrow," he said, and he explained why. "I have no idea what your position is at this moment. I'm certainly not going to ask for a decision while you're on the telephone. But talk this over with your father. Tell him thanks for what he's already done to help. Then let's see what happens."

September the tenth arrived.

The morning mail came—envelopes from children sending in their coins.

"Thank You, Lord," I said. "We couldn't do without these."

The morning chapel service began. Everyone prayed and sang. Here and there I heard our young people thanking God for sending us the check for $15,000.

In the middle of the service, I was called to the door.

It was a special delivery. I looked at the postmark: Chicago, Illinois.

I opened the envelope, and inside was a certified check for exactly $15,000.

I couldn't talk when I took that piece of paper into the chapel. I stood before the fireplace with its sheaf of harvested wheat in bas-relief on the mantel. I held up my hand for silence, and when the room was quiet, Paul DiLena handed the check to the young boy nearest me.

"Pass that around, will you please?" Paul said.

The canceled check, which Clem Stone now has in his files in Chicago, tells a mute story of the wonderful leading of God among young people in New York City. It is properly endorsed, properly deposited.

But if you look closely at that check, you will see that it is stained—grubby, really, from having passed through the hands of two dozen youngsters who had learned what it is to believe. Perhaps there are some tearstains on it, too. Tears of gratitude to a God who moves in mysterious ways His wonders to perform.

For decades Reverend David Wilkerson was known for his work among teen gangs in New York City. His book *The Cross and the Switchblade* has sold millions of copies worldwide and was made into a feature film. He authored more than forty books and was also the inspiration behind Nicky Cruz's book, *Run Baby Run*. Reverend Wilkerson passed away in 2011.

Elizabeth and John Sherrill met as young people on board the *Queen Elizabeth* and were married in Switzerland. Together they have written more than thirty books, including *The Cross and the Switchblade* with David Wilkerson, *God's Smuggler* with Brother Andrew, and *The Hiding Place* with Corrie ten Boom. The Sherrills' writing has taken them to five continents, reporting the Holy Spirit's awe-inspiring deeds into the 21st century. John Sherrill passed away in 2017.

More Exciting, Beautifully Illustrated True Stories for Young Readers!

It's World War II. Darkness has fallen over Europe as the Nazis spread hatred, fear and war across the globe. But on a quiet city corner in the Netherlands, one woman fights against the darkness. This is her remarkable story of heroism and faith that will inspire a new generation of readers with a timeless message.

The Hiding Place, Young Reader's Edition by Corrie ten Boom, John and Elizabeth Sherrill

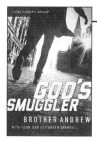

It's the Cold War, and fear rules Eastern Europe, where all talk of God is against the law. Yet one unlikely man, armed only with God's Word and His protection, refuses to give in to tyranny. This is his exciting story. Join Brother Andrew for the adventure of a lifetime and see for yourself how God always makes a way for those who trust in Him.

God's Smuggler, Young Reader's Edition by Brother Andrew, John and Elizabeth Sherrill

✔Chosen

Stay up to date on your favorite books and authors with our free e-newsletters. Sign up today at chosenbooks.com.

Find us on Facebook. facebook.com/chosenbooks

Follow us on Twitter. @Chosen_Books